Avadhuta Gita

Song of the Liberated Soul

Translation and Commentary by Rory B Mackay

Copyright © Rory B. Mackay, 2022

First Edition

Published by Blue Star Publishing

UnbrokenSelf.com

Cover and interior design by Rory Mackay

The right of Rory B. Mackay to be identified as the author of this work has been asserted by him in accordance with the Copyright, Designs and Patents Act, 1988. All rights reserved. No part of this publication may be reproduced, distributed or transmitted in any form or by any means without prior written permission.

Avadhuta Gita: Song of the Liberated Soul / Rory B. Mackay — 1st ed.
ISBN 978-1-7396089-0-3

For Ramji and Sundari.

Contents

Introduction 1

Chapter One 5

Chapter Two 33

Chapter Three 55

Chapter Four 71

Chapter Five 81

Chapter Six 95

Chapter Seven 111

Introduction

The Avadhuta Gita is a short and poetic Vedantic text condensed into seven chapters. (An eight chapter exists but is generally believed to be a later and, in this author's view, inessential addition to the text.)

Admittedly, it is not the ideal introduction for those new to Vedanta. It doesn't expound the logic of the teaching, nor elaborate much upon its grand pronouncements. What it does is provide insight into the perspective of an enlightened mind; the mind of one who has pierced the veil of Self-ignorance and is fully cognisant of the Absolute, Non-dual nature of Existence.

The term *avadhuta* refers to one who has transcended all worldly identifications and who lives freely and without bondage, craving or attachment. Such a soul has attained what we call enlightenment—which, in simple terms, means the shifting of our identity from the ego-self to the one, formless, all-pervading Awareness or Consciousness that animates and sustains all beings.

Unhindered by Self-ignorance and its resultant sense of separation, lack, desire and attachment, the avadhuta is free to live life on his or her own terms. Such a Self-Realised being no longer identifies with the adjuncts of body, mind, intellect and ego, and sees no separation between themselves and God, or the various forms of the world. This is what the mystics call 'God consciousness' or 'Unity consciousness'. Vedanta simply calls it *moksha*, or liberation.

No longer dependent upon the ever-shifting forms of the world for their happiness, the liberated have no set rules. They may exist as yogis or ascetics, content to wander the countryside in utter nakedness. Or they may live as householders and hold down a job and family, outwardly appearing little different to anyone else.

Inwardly, however, things are as different as night and day. Unencumbered by a false ego-identity, and no longer taking themselves to be a finite entity subject to time, limitation and death, such a person's mind is forever merged in its Source: the eternal, ever-free Reality that is Brahman, the Self, or pure Awareness.

The word *gita* means "song". This text is, therefore, the song of the enlightened one or the liberated soul. You might look upon the concise, pithy statements of each verse as the exaltations of a mind freed from bondage.

There is little in the way of sequential progression to the verses, and they alternate between statements of Indirect and Direct Knowledge. Indirect Knowledge means knowing the Self as an object; as That which is to be known. Direct Knowledge means owning one's identity as the Self, and referring to it as "I am"; as That which is me; both the Knower and the known. One verse may speak of the Self in first person terms ("I am the Self"), while the next might refer to it in the second person ("you are the Self"). Both refer the one, universal Self—pure unconditioned Consciousness—the essence and substrate of Existence. This one Self illumines and enlivens every body and mind, just as the same sun shines through countless windows.

As with many Vedantic texts, the authorship of the Avadhuta Gita is open to debate, although it is attributed to the great sage Dattatreya, a quasi-mythical figure believed to be an incarnation of Vishnu. The exact dating is disputed. Some suggest that it may have been composed around the 9th century, after the time of Adi Shankaracharya. Others believe, however, that it may have been passed down orally for centuries beforehand.

INTRODUCTION

Artist's Impression of the Sage Dattatreya

A perfect text for meditation and deep contemplation, the Avadhuta Gita has inspired seekers and the enlightened alike for centuries. I have endeavoured to maintain fidelity to the original Sanskrit while keeping the translation accessible and clear, and hopefully conveying its poeticism and eloquence. I would like to acknowledge the 1992 translation of Swami Abhayananda as being a particular inspiration.

While the text more than speaks for itself, I have provided commentary on select verses to elaborate upon certain ideas and resolve any potential confusion that might arise.

Om Tat Sat.

Chapter One

1. By Divine grace, the enlightened come to know the Truth of Non-duality, realising the unity of all things. This knowledge liberates the mind from great fear.

Why would the knowledge of Non-duality free the mind from fear? Fear is born of misidentification; of assuming ourselves to be what we are not. Owing to self-ignorance and taking appearance to be real, we believe ourselves to be nothing but a limited body-mind-ego entity. This fundamental misperception of reality lies at the root of humankind's ingrained sense of separation and limitation.

Fear arises because what is finite is always subject to injury, death and cessation. At the level of form, there's simply no way around this predicament. The only solution to the problem of existential fear is to inquire into the nature of the Self and reality. If fear is caused by the false notion of duality, which originates in the mind, then the only remedy, as we shall see, is to re-educate the mind with the Knowledge of Non-duality.

In the words of the Taittiriya Upanishad:

"When one realises the Self, in whom all life is changeless, nameless and formless, then one fears no more. Until we realise the unity of life, we live in fear."

2. All that exists is the Self, and the Self alone. Blissful, indestructible and all-pervading, it cannot be separated from Itself. How, then, shall the Infinite worship Itself? Shiva is the undivided whole!

In the Avadhuta Gita, the term Shiva doesn't refer to a specific deity as such, but to the eternal, formless and boundless Self. In its broadest sense, the word Shiva means "That which is always auspicious and all-pervading." As the Absolute Reality pervading all things, Shiva is everything, everywhere. That being so, there is nothing It is not.

3. The world appears in Me like a desert mirage. To whom shall I bow? As pure Awareness, I alone am; free of impurity and untarnished by anything in this world.

Here we come to an important question. If, as the scriptures declare, the Self is an undivided whole—Infinite, without limit and without beginning or end—how can we explain this universe of finitude and duality?

According to Advaita Vedanta, this world of duality appears superimposed within the Self courtesy of *maya*. Maya is the inexplicable power within Awareness that creates the appearance of separation and duality within the Non-dual ground of pure, divisionless Being. Thus, within the formless Unmanifest, an entire universe of form and differentiation comes into apparent existence, much as a world of dreams appears in your mind each night as you sleep.

Just as you, the dreamer, are unaffected by the content of your dreams, no matter how wondrous or terrifying they might be, so, too, is the all-pervading Self unaffected by anything in this universe of form. From the perspective of the Self, it is appearance only and as unreal as the water of a desert mirage.

4. All that exists is the Self. Neither divided nor undivided, it defies categorisation. I can only speak of it with wonder and awe!

How can we speak of the Infinite? Using words to describe what is ultimately beyond words can only ever be a crude superimposition. The Infinite is said to be devoid of characteristics, because characteristics of any kind would require form, and form necessitates limitation.

5. The supreme truth of Vedanta, the Highest of all Knowledge, is simply this: I am the Self, the limitless Awareness pervading all things.

The full integration of this Knowledge is the key to *moksha*, or enlightenment. Enlightenment means liberation from suffering. If suffering is caused by identification with the finite, with maya's realm of names and forms, liberation is attained by realising our identity as, and non-separation from, the Infinite. You might think of a sentient wave suddenly realising that it isn't, in fact, a separate, self-existent and time-bound form, but is actually non-separate from the vast ocean pervading it. What relief; what wonder!

6. Neither constricted nor contained, I am the Self in all; the light shining within the heart of all beings. I am formless like the cloudless sky, unchanging, ever-pure and stainless.

7. Infinite and imperishable, I am pure Awareness without form. I am untouched by either joy or sorrow.

Joy and sorrow pertain to the mind, just as pleasure and pain pertain to the body. While the body and mind are experienced by the light of Awareness, Awareness, which is your own Self, remains free of both.

8. The actions of the mind, body and tongue, whether good or bad, do not affect me. Beyond the senses, I am the pure nectar of Self-knowledge.

It's crucial to understand that although the body and mind are subject to modification and both pleasure and pain, the Self is unaffected, for it is subtler than the mind, body and senses. To know this beyond a shadow of a doubt is to be liberated from bondage.

9. The mind is formless like space, yet it wears a million faces. Within it appear images from the past and worldly forms. Awareness, however—the essence of what I am—exists apart from the mind and remains unaffected by it.

10. As the Self, I am the one Existence; I am everything everywhere! Although appearing as multiplicity, I am undifferentiated and pervade all forms. As the Self, I am both the Unmanifest and the manifest; the seer and the seen.

11. You, also, are the one Existence! Why don't you understand? You are the unchanging Self, the same shining consciousness that enlivens all beings equally. Limitless and indestructible, you are the all-pervading Light. For this ever-shining Light, there can be no distinction between day and night.

The Self is both self-existent and self-effulgent. Of the nature of Awareness or pure Consciousness, it is the light that has no opposite; for it is eternal and needs no other illumination to reveal it. Because this all-pervading Awareness shines eternally, it has neither beginning nor end. By its light, all the objects of the mind and senses are revealed and known.

12. The Self is continuous, unbroken and changeless. The One within all, It knows no division. This "I" is both the subject and the supreme object of meditation. How can one divide the indivisible?

13. You, O Self, were never born and will never die. Birth and death do not pertain to You. You have never been a body. As the scriptures state in many ways: "All is Brahman"; all is Limitless and Eternal Awareness.

The Self doesn't appear in a body; rather, the body appears in the Self. Were you to analyse your own direct experience, you would have to conclude that all objects, whether tangible material objects or the subtle objects of thought and imagination, appear in Awareness and are ultimately indivisible from Awareness. Awareness is the substrate and essence of all that is perceivable. Try though you might, you can never divorce Awareness from the objects it perceives.

14. You are That which is both within and without. You are Shiva; you are everything everywhere! Why, then, is your mind so deluded? Why do you run about like a frightened ghost?

Self-ignorance causes us to rush about the world like desperate phantoms. Driven by an inherent sense of lack and incompleteness, we find ourselves hungrily devouring objects of sensory experience in a desperate bid to remove this deep-rooted feeling of incompleteness. A mind subject to Self-ignorance is naturally a troubled, disturbed mind; a mind caught in the unrelenting grasp of *samsara*.

Buddhists speak of the realm of "hungry ghosts". These wraith-like spectres are said to be constantly ravenous and desperate to keep consuming experience. Tragically, however, they have only pinhole mouths. As a result, no matter how hard they try, they can never satisfy their hunger. This metaphor perfectly describes the state of samsara, as experienced to varying degrees by almost every human being.

The key is plain to see in this verse. Dattatreya is addressing the mind. That's where the problem lies. Ignorance is a product of the mind and the only solution is, therefore, to re-educate the mind.

15. Neither union or separation exist for you or me. There is ultimately no "you", no "me", and no universe about us. All is the Self alone.

All the waves in the ocean are nothing but water assuming a temporary time-bound form. Likewise, the universe and all the beings within it are nothing but the Self assuming a temporary time-bound form.

16. As Awareness, you cannot be be heard, or smelled, or tasted; nor can you be seen, or sensed by touch. Beyond the five senses, you are the Ultimate, all encompassing Reality. Why, then, do you suffer so?

The message of the Upanishads is simply this: To know yourself as you truly are is to go beyond suffering. Nothing in the world of form and experience can then touch or taint you any more than the fevered imaginings of the dreamer can affect the person dreaming.

17. Neither birth or death, nor bondage or liberation affect you at all. They exist in the mind, but not in You. Why then, my friend, are you crying? We are beyond name and form.

18. O mind, why do you flit about like a restless ghost? Realise the indivisible Self! Relinquish this attachment and false identification, and be happy and free!

When you believe yourself to be a finite entity with a deeply ingrained sense of lack and incompleteness, how can you ever be happy and free? Simply put, you cannot.

As long as you remain identified with the adjuncts of the body and mind—their woes are your woes. On the other hand, when you see them as simply objects appearing in the vast Awareness that you are, their properties no longer belong to you, and neither do their sorrows.

19. You are the changeless Truth and Essence of everything; the Eternal One; indomitable, boundless and ever free from modification. Neither attachment nor aversion belong to you. Why, then, do you entertain thoughts of limitation and succumb to desire?

Assimilating the knowledge "I am the Self; pure, limitless Awareness" will almost certainly take time. After all, the mind has been accustomed to thinking in terms of duality and limitation for decades; even lifetimes. Until this Knowledge is fully internalised, you will likely continue experiencing the mind's same old patterns of limitation along with its ingrained desires and aversions.

Rather than seeing this as a bad thing, you can use it as a helpful gauge as to how firm your Self-Knowledge is. With time and the repeated application of Self-Knowledge to the mind, you'll eventually find the old patterns of ignorance, self-limitation and craving fading away like darkness in the morning light.

20. The Vedantic scriptures unanimously declare the Self to be the pure, formless, imperishable Awareness that is essence of all forms. Know That to be your true nature beyond any doubt.

21. All forms, whether gross or subtle, are but temporary manifestations. Only the formless Reality pervading them is eternal. To realise this Truth is to pass beyond birth and death.

22. The Self, the One Reality, is ever the same; so say the great Sages. When you relinquish desire and attachment, the mind sees neither duality or unity.

Duality doesn't exist outside of the mind. Reality is an undivided Whole. The mind, however, believing only the visible to be real and, taking itself to be a separate body/mind/ego, functions by breaking reality into bitesize pieces, labelling and categorising each. It thus creates an entire universe of "this" and "that"; "me" and "not-me".

Falling for what Einstein called this "optical delusion of consciousness"—and believing ourselves to be separate, isolated and incomplete entities—our delusion binds us to desire and attachment, further deluding the mind. A deluded mind is incapable of interfacing with reality with any measure of clarity and inevitably leads us ever deeper into the bondage of samsara.

23. If you seek the Self in the unreal world of objects, how can you know the unity of existence? If you see the world as other than the Self, how can you know the unity of existence? True liberation is knowing everything as One.

24. When you realise yourself to be the pure and imperishable Reality—without birth, without body, and the same in all beings—how can you then say, "I know the Self" or "I don't know the Self"?

For the enlightened, talk of the Self is unnecessary and redundant. It is enough to simply *be* the Self.

25. The Vedantic proclamation Tat tvam asi, "That thou art", affirms the true nature of your identity as the Self. The saying neti neti, "not this, not this", negates the reality of the world of the five elements.

One of the essential tools of Vedantic practice is learning to discriminate the Self from the "not-Self", or the Real from the only apparently real. The upshot is that anything known to you as an object, whether gross or subtle—whether an outer form or the form of a thought, memory, emotion, and so on—cannot *be* you.

As the Self, you are never available as an object of perception because you are the eternal Subject; the boundless Awareness in which all objects arise and subside and by which they are known. You are the eternal Knower; always present, ever existent, yet never available for objectification. The real crux of spiritual practice is simply learning to discriminate between you, Awareness, and the ephemeral objects appearing in you.

26. The Self is the true identity of all; It contains and pervades this entire universe. Your very nature is fullness, for you are everything; the unbroken whole. For the Self, there is no thinker and no object of thought. Why then, O mind, do you go on thinking so shamelessly?

The Indian sage Tilopa once stated that the way to liberation was to "Cut the mind at its root and rest in naked awareness."

The human mind is designed to keep us safe and, as an extension of that, to guard and enhance our egoic self-concept. Vedantic meditation is continuously bringing the mind back to its Source, pure Awareness, allowing for the full assimilation of the Knowledge "I am Awareness".

As pure Awareness, you have nothing to gain, nothing to lose, and nothing to acquire, protect or fear. A mind fully cognisant of this truth naturally begins to quieten; its grasping attachments and fitful anxieties melting like snow in the sunlight. This process of taming the mind can only be achieved by the consistent and rigorous application of Self-Knowledge.

27. If I know not Shiva, how can I speak of Him? If I know not Shiva, how can I worship It? I am Shiva! The primal Essence of all; my nature, boundless like the sky, remains ever the same.

28. As the all-pervading Essence of all forms, I have no form of my own. I am beyond the division of subject and object. How could I possibly be an object to myself?

As the Self, you are pure Awareness; the eternal Subject. Always present and forever shining, Awareness is always the Knower and never the known. Just as a camera can photograph anything but itself, the Self enables the mind to perceive anything but is never itself an object of perception.

Some people are unsatisfied with this because they believe they want to '"experience the Self". However, there is never any time that you are *not* experiencing the Self. It is the very medium by which you experience reality. It's impossible to divorce the objects of Awareness from Awareness itself. Therefore, there's never a time that you aren't experiencing the Self. Because Awareness is subtler than the objects it illumines, you may simply not be aware of that Awareness, even though it is the very foundation of your entire existence.

29. Though wearing the guise of countless forms, the Infinite Reality has no form of its own. The one Self, the Highest Truth, is limitless. Nothing else exists. Actionless, the Self neither creates, sustains nor destroys anything.

Action pertains to maya, the world of the objects, which appears in the Self much as a dream appears in the sleeping mind. Just as the sun shines upon the world, allowing life to flourish while itself uninvolved and actionless, the Self is that which allows the maya world to exist and function, while remaining actionless and unchanged by it.

30. As the pure and changeless Essence; you are beyond form; birthless and deathless. For you, how could such a thing as delusion exist? Delusion cannot exist for the Infinite.

Ignorance is a product of the mind alone and never touches or changes the Self in any way. As the mind is the source of our Self-ignorance, the solution is to remedy this with the application of Self-Knowledge. No matter the state of the mind, whether enlightened or unenlightened, the Self is always free. That's why delusion and illumination relate to the mind only—and not you, as the ever free Self.

31. When a glass jar is broken, the space within unites with the space around it. Similarly, when the mind is purified, it sees no difference between itself and Shiva, the Eternal Self.

Enlightenment isn't a process of gain. It's not about acquiring or "adding" anything to yourself in any way. It's not an event or a process of becoming. It's simply the result of Knowledge: the Knowledge that you are already whole and non-different from the pure, unchanging, taintless Awareness/Consciousness that is Self.

32. From the perspective of the Absolute, there is no jar and neither inner nor outer space. There is no body and no individual to lay claim to it. Everything is the One Indivisible Self. There is no subject, no object, and no separate parts.

33. Eternal and ever present in all things, the Self alone exists. The world of form, both Unmanifest and manifest, is nothing but my Self. Of this, I have no doubt!

34. For the Self, there are no scriptures, no world, and no rituals or offerings. There are no gods, nor classes, nor races of men; no stages of life, and no path of darkness or path of light. There is nothing but pure Awareness, the supreme Reality and highest Truth.

35. The subject and object are one and the same, and you are That eternal, non-dual One. This being so, with no existent "other", how can the Self be perceived as an object?

36. Some seek Non-duality, while others remain content with duality. They don't understand that the all-pervading Reality is beyond duality and non-duality.

To speak of Non-duality infers the existence of duality. Duality doesn't exist outside of the mind. It exists in perception alone. The Self is beyond both duality and Non-duality because it is the eternal One without a second. It is the single existent factor in reality. In spite of appearances to the contrary, there is nothing other than it, so, for the enlightened, talk of duality and Non-duality is redundant.

37. How can one describe the supreme Reality when it has no colour, no sound, or qualities of any kind? How can one think or speak of that which is beyond the range of thought or speech?

Vedanta teaches by a process of superimposition and negation (*adhyaropa apavada*). For the purposes of teaching, we may ascribe certain qualities or attributes to the Self, but we later retract them by revealing that the ultimate Reality is beyond description and categorisation. It simply *is*.

38. When you know this world of form to be as vast and empty as the sky, then you will know the Self and pierce the veil of duality.

We come to realise the Real by negating the unreal.

39. With Indirect Knowledge, the Self appears to be other than I. With Direct Knowledge, I know it to be that which I am. Undivided like space, the Self alone exists. How, then, can the subject and object of meditation be separate?

The initial stages of teaching reveal the Self via Indirect Knowledge, as an object known to us—hence, we talk of "the Self". As we begin to covert Indirect Knowledge to Direct Knowledge, we claim ownership of it. It's no longer "the Self", but "my Self". After all, if the Self is everything, then what else can it be? What started as an abstract object is now firmly understood to be the eternal Subject; the very essence and totality of what we are.

40. I do not act, eat, give or take, for I am the Self. As the Self, I am actionless, pure, and beyond birth and death.

Pivotal to enlightenment is the realisation that, as the Self, you are actionless. The Self doesn't act, although all actions happen by the grace of its existence. A helpful metaphor is to think of the sun. It is by virtue of the heat and light of the sun that life on Earth can exist and flourish. In many respects, the sun is the source of all life on our planet, yet it never performs any action itself other than existing and shining its light.

41. Know the whole of the universe to be without form. Know the whole of the universe to be without change. Know the whole of the universe to be pure and untouched by its contents. Know the whole of the universe to be the embodiment of Shiva.

Here, the "whole" refers to the Absolute order of reality; the ground of Existence which is the Self, or Shiva. In Vedanta terminology, we call this *paramartika satyam*, which means the absolute order of existence—the immaterial, boundless substratum in which the phenomenal universe appears as an objective world of form and experience (*vyavaharika satyam*). This objective world depends upon the Absolute for its existence just as the waves depend upon the ocean for their existence. After all, an effect cannot exist independently of its cause.

42. Know yourself to be the Ultimate Reality, and have no doubt. The Self is not something that can be known by the mind, for the Self is that by which the mind is known. How can you seek to know what you already are?

43. O dear one, why get so absorbed in the material universe? Whether the shadow is present or not, it has no independent reality. Existence is One. The Ultimate Reality is everything everywhere; all-pervading and free like space. Nothing else exists.

44. I am without beginning, middle or end. I am not bound, nor will I ever be. By my very nature, I am stainless, whole and pure. This I know with certainty.

45. From the subtlest of elements to the gross forms of the universe, all that exists is the Self alone. The stages of life and divisions of society have no meaning to me.

46. I see everything as the One Indivisible Reality. This undivided One constitutes the void, all of space, and the world of the senses and the five elements.

47. The world of manifold form is simply an appearance in the One Universal Awareness that is the Self. In spite of appearances, there is only one factor in existence, and that is the Self.

48. The Self is neither male, female, nor neuter. It possesses neither intellect nor the power of thought. How can you imagine it to possess form and distinction when it is the Essence of all things?

49. Practising yoga will not lead you to purity. Neither will emptying the mind of all thoughts, or following the teachings of a guru. As the immortal Self, you are, by your very nature, pure, Eternal Awareness.

Although spiritual teachings often speak in terms of attainment, the Self is not something you can attain. It is already attained. It is not something you can add to yourself or a state of consciousness you can manufacture. You are already the totality of Existence. The practise of yoga, meditation and the teaching of Vedanta cannot "add" that to you. They are simply tools for freeing the mind of Self-ignorance. When you remove that ignorance, the light of Truth alone remains.

50. Neither the gross body of the five elements, nor the subtle body of mind, intellect, and ego, have any independent reality. Only the Self has independent and lasting existence. All states of consciousness are but appearances in the Self.

In Vedanta, anything objectifiable by the mind and senses falls into the category of *mithya*. Mithya means that which is only apparently real; that which has no inherent existence of its own. Gold rings, ornaments and bangles are all examples of mithya. These objects have a name and form and are experienceable by the senses, but they have no independent existence of their own. The "ring", for instance, doesn't exist separately from the gold—it is simply gold in a certain shape and form. If you melt it down, the "ring" will be lost but the gold will remain because it exists independently of the ring.

In the same way, this entire universe of name and form has no independent existence of its own. It is mithya; an effect dependent on an underlying cause—namely, pure Awareness or Consciousness (terms we use synonymously). The forms of the world are entirely dependent upon the Essence from which they arise and subside—and that essence is Universal Awareness.

50. I am neither bound nor am I liberated. I am neither the doer nor the enjoyer of action. I am pure Awareness and nothing else. I do not pervade, nor am I pervaded.

Vedantic scriptures talk of the Self as being "all-pervading" like space. Dattatreya appears to contradict that in the final sentence of this verse. This is simply a shift of perspective. From the perspective of maya, it helps to think of the Self as the Essence pervading all things. But from the perspective of the Self, It doesn't pervade anything. Why? Because there is nothing other than It—and, therefore, nothing to pervade.

51. When ice and water are mixed, they become one without distinction. Similarly, in combination, prakriti and purusha, matter and spirit, are indistinguishable from each other.

The terms *prakriti* and *purusha* refer to the principles of matter and spirit; the seen and the unseen, or the objects and the Awareness in which they appear.

The two are "indistinguishable" because, in order to experience anything, both principles must be present. You can never experience the objective phenomenal world without Awareness. Awareness is That by which all forms are perceived and That from which they borrow their existence. Therefore, to exist and function in the world, both these factors must combine to create the universe of form and experience.

52. Having never been bound, I need never be liberated. How could the Self, with or without form, ever be bound?

53. The Supreme Self, the mother of all things, exists everywhere like space. The world of form appears in it like the water of a desert mirage.

The world of maya, of form and differentiation, appears in the Self, Awareness, much as a dream appears in the mind of the dreamer (or, to use the example here, a mirage in the mind of a desert traveller). The dreamer pervades the entire dream; there is nowhere and nothing he or she is not. While the dream isn't real, you can't claim that it doesn't exist, for it is clearly experienced by the mind and the inward turned senses. Rather, like the sand mistaken for a desert oasis, it appears to exist at some level, but is not real.

54. I have neither guru nor teaching and no action to perform. I am, by my very nature, as pure and as free as the formless sky.

55. You are the self-existent purity. Neither body nor mind pertain to you. You are the Supreme Reality. Do not be ashamed to declare, "I am the Self, the Supreme Reality!"

56. Why do you weep, O mind? Realise the Self, beloved. Drink the timeless nectar of Non-duality.

Our sorrows are always born of self-misapprehension. By taking appearance to be real, we have assumed ourselves to be a limited body-mind entity subject to all manner of suffering, pain and eventual death. When our perspective shifts to the Awareness in which the body and mind arise, we realise ourselves to be unbounded and free. By shifting perspective, the mind no longer has cause to grieve.

57. Knowledge does not pertain to you, nor ignorance; nor a mixture of the two. You, yourself, are the essence of Knowledge; a Self-existent Knowledge that never ceases or errs.

58. I am not knowledge born of the intellect, nor am I attained by deep meditation or yoga. I am not gained by the passage of time or by the guru's instruction. My nature is pure Awareness; the highest Truth and ultimate Reality. Though I may appear to change with time, I am like space; ever changeless and free.

59. As I have no birth, I have no death. I perform no action, either good or bad. I am Awareness; pure and free of all qualities. How can bondage or liberation exist for that which has no form?

60. If the Self is all-pervading, eternal, whole, and without division, there can be no differentiation whatsoever. How, then, can it be regarded as being either "inside" or "outside"?

61. The entire universe shines as One; inseparable, divisionless and partless. Belief in the independent existence of maya is a great delusion. Duality and Non-duality are mere concepts of the mind.

62. The world of form, which has no independent existence, cannot be separated from the formless in which it appears. How can there be either division or union when there is nothing but the Self alone?

63. You have no mother or father, nor brother, spouse, child, or friend. You are unaffected by attachment or impartiality. Why, then, is your mind so perturbed?

Relationship troubles disappear the instant you realise that, as the One without a second, there is only You! Everyone you ever encounter is but an expression of the one Consciousness; the same sun reflected upon all the mirrors in all the world.

64. O mind, there is neither day nor night, creation nor dissolution. The light of the Self is continuous and never rises or sets. How can the wise possibly believe that the formless Self can in any way be affected by the world of form?

Ordinarily, the process of creation involves a change in the underlying substance. For instance, when milk is churned into butter it undergoes an irreversible change and will never be milk again.

However, although the maya world is a product of the Self in much the same way heat is a product of fire, the Self is unaffected by this creation. The creation appears, but the Self remains unchanged. This is because the Self is of a different order of reality to the manifest world. What happens in one order of reality is specific to that level and can't affect any other order of reality. For example, even though you might dream that you've won the lottery, when you wake up in the morning you won't bother trying to claim your prize. This is because the lottery win only pertained to the dream order of reality; it doesn't impact the waking order of reality whatsoever. Just as the waking world is unaffected by the world of your dreams, the Self is unaffected by the world of maya.

65. It is neither divided nor undivided. It experiences neither sorrow nor joy. It is neither the universe, nor is it not the universe. The Self is the eternal, imperishable One.

66. I am not the doer, nor am I the enjoyer. I am unbound by karma, past or present. I have no body, nor am I bodiless. Therefore, how can a sense of possession, of "mine" or "not mine", be assigned to Me?

With the assimilation of Self-Knowledge comes the negation of your sense of doership and ownership. The Self—being the totality of everything; divisionless, actionless and ever whole—can have no sense of ownership; of "me" or "mine", because there is nothing other than it. The notion of possession is meaningless when there is no other.

67. I am uncontaminated by passions or attachment, nor do I suffer from bodily afflictions. Know me to be the one Self; as vast and endless as the open sky.

68. O mind, my friend, what is the use of so much vain talk? O mind, my friend, what is to gain by such fruitless wrangling? I have told you the highest Truth: You are the ultimate Reality. You are unbound and free like space.

Enlightenment is basically the re-education of the mind. Rather than identifying as a body-mind entity, as has been the mind's default setting, your centre of identification shifts to Awareness. This rarely happens overnight, for it requires the steady and consistent application of Self-Knowledge to the errant mind. In Vedanta, the term for this re-education of the mind is *nididhyasana*. For it to work, all your thoughts, beliefs and habitual reactions must be examined as they arise and held up to the light of Truth: the Knowledge that you are whole, ever-free Awareness. Without this process of mental reeducation, the formations of the mind will continue to be conditioned by the mind's old patterns of ignorance.

69. In whatever place and in whatever state a yogi dies, his consciousness is absorbed into the Absolute, just as the space inside a jar unites with the space around it when the jar is broken.

70. Whether he dies at a holy place or in a lowly hut, the yogi, having divested himself of all bodily identification, realises his non-separation from the Absolute pervading all.

This and the previous verse explore what happens when the Self-Realised person sheds their body. Because they have realised their identity as the Self, they have negated their karma. Karma belongs to the world of maya, whereas the transcendent Self is ever untouched by maya.

The Self was never actually bound in any way. A false identification lay at the root of our bondage; a sense of doership and ownership—specifically, believing ourselves to be a body/mind/ego subject to birth, death and karma. When this ignorance is destroyed, our "karmic account" is closed, so to speak; and, in the absence of karma, no further birth is necessary.

71. To the enlightened, righteousness, action, the pursuit of wealth, pleasure and liberation–and all the people and objects in the world–are as illusory as the water of a desert mirage.

The wise see the objects of the world for what they are: maya—a dependent effect resulting from an independent cause: ie., the Self. The world and all the objects in it certainly exist, but, just as a dream has no any existence outside of the dreamer, they have no inherent existence of their own.

72. As the Self, I perform no action. No action, past or present, was ever undertaken or enjoyed by Me. This I know beyond all doubt.

73. The liberated soul, aware that all is but his own Self, lives alone, always content, and moves about the world, open-hearted, happy and free.

As long as you believe your happiness to be dependent upon external factors you'll inevitably experience a lifetime of anxiety and sorrow. Only when you realise that happiness and freedom are inherent to your very nature can you breathe easy and begin to enjoy life for what it is.

The enlightened know there's nothing to gain in the world and nothing to lose either. With this comes an incredible sense of detachment and fearlessness as you realise that there's nothing that you can't do in life. Life ceases to be a relentless struggle to "make things work" and "become somebody" and instead becomes a celebration of gratitude and wonder.

74. States of consciousness, whether exalted or mundane, are irrelevant when all is experienced as the Self alone. When neither dharma nor adharma pertain, how could you experience either bondage or liberation?

The dualistic yogic notion of the Self as a "state of consciousness" that can be attained or added to you is a huge obstacle to Self-

Knowledge. It has kept sincere and ardent seekers locked in ignorance, misplaced effort and frustration throughout the ages. The Self is limitless and eternal, therefore, there's nothing other than it. So, whatever state of consciousness you are experiencing right now can only be the Self. In fact, the Self is that by which all states of consciousness are experienced and known. You can never *not* be experiencing the Self. All that's missing is true knowledge of the Self: the knowledge that you are already whole, complete and free—and this knowledge is attained by removing the mind's ignorance.

75. The liberated being, having assimilated the knowledge of their own essential nature, declares that neither the mantras of scripture nor the practices of tantra can ever adequately reveal the Self.

76. It is meaningless to differentiate between the void and the world of form. It is pointless to speak of the "real "and "the unreal". All that exists is the One, unchanging, Eternal Self. That is the declaration of the scriptures.

Chapter 2

1. Although a person may be young, immature, addicted to sense pleasure, a householder or a servant, everyone has the capacity to teach Knowledge. The value of a diamond is not lost simply because it is encrusted with some mud.

2. A teacher may lack standard education and literary skill. Such qualities are not required. Take the Truth they teach and ignore all else. An unpainted, unadorned boat will carry you across the river just as well as an embellished vessel.

The message of this and the preceding verse is that in maya, all things are imperfect. Perfected beings (which is to say, Self-Realised people with highly refined minds) are astonishingly rare, particularly in our modern age. If you are intent on waiting for an objectively perfect teacher, replete with glowing halo, you're likely to be in for a long wait.

It is, of course, essential to be discriminating and judicious when it comes to spiritual teachers. There are many false gurus and exploitative individuals out there ready to abuse their position in order to feed their narcissism and lustful appetites. But once you have found a qualified teacher, and one who lives what they teach and is committed to helping rather than exploiting others (whether monetarily or in any other way), take what they teach and seek to actualise it.

A teacher should be honoured and respected, but they should never be put on a pedestal and idolised. In the Vedantic teaching tradition, the relationship between teacher and student is one of friendship and mutual respect. The focus should not be the glorification of the teacher, but the glorification of the Knowledge that he or she shares. As this verse states, the guru is simply a vessel; one capable of taking you from a place of darkness (ignorance) to a place of light (knowledge).

The very word *guru* means "remover of darkness". It's not necessary for that vessel to be adorned with bells and whistles, or to have the grandest of followings. The enlightened are often unobtrusive people. They don't go out of their way to seek the limelight or court attention because they are already whole and complete in themselves. Accordingly, often the greatest of souls and best of teachers are very humble and ordinary. Be sure not to miss them simply because you're looking for some media-savvy guru with a million-dollar "spiritual" empire.

3. Without any effort whatsoever, the immutable Self pervades and sustains the worlds of both the animate and inanimate. Its nature is pure, unconditioned Awareness, ever at peace and as expansive as the heavens.

There's no effort for the Self, for It is the totality of all that is; the substance, support and essence of all things. Awareness pervades all as the very substratum of existence. Nothing is capable of touching it and nothing can affect it in any way. To know yourself as that Awareness—which isn't some exalted state of consciousness, but the everyday, ordinary, ever present awareness illuming all your senses, thoughts and experiences—is to know freedom.

4. Appearing as the worlds of the animate and inanimate, and governing them without the least effort, the Self is forever one. How can that which is limitless and all-pervading be subject to division or duality? How can this Eternal Self be anything other than "I"?

The very heart of Vedanta can be encapsulated by three short words: *Tat tvam asi*, or "That I am". *Tat*, or That, refers to the Self; pure limitless Consciousness/Awareness. In this context, "I" refers to what we call the jiva; the body/mind/ego; the sense of being a separate and autonomous being. The final word in the equation, "am", expresses the non-separation between the two. In actuality, there is no jiva. The jiva is just a conglomeration of gross and subtle matter which, courtesy of self-ignorance is taken to be oneself.

The first two stages of Vedanta, listening (*shravana*) and reasoning (*manana*), provide knowledge of the Self. The third stage, *nididhyasana*, involves claiming ownership of that Self through consistent contemplation and Self-inquiry. You no longer speak of the Self as an object; as something that is known by you. To speak *of* the Self is Indirect Knowledge. By clearly knowing that you *are* the Self, and claiming it as "I", you convert this Indirect Knowledge to Direct Knowledge. Accordingly, the next few verses speak of the Self not in the third person as an object ("the Self") but in the first person ("I").

5. This "I", indeed, is the Highest Truth: the Eternal Self, in which all worlds, whether tangible or intangible, appear. Subtler than the subtlest of elements, I neither come, nor do I go. Formless, I am beyond all states and am not subject to modification.

The Self is the Eternal Knower; the substratum of Awareness in which all conceivable objects and experiences are known—from the gross world of tangible form to the subtle world of thought and dreams. Yet, being subtler than any object of experience, this Awareness is never affected by those forms and experiences in any way.

6. Being formless in nature, I am, therefore, free of all constituent parts. The highest of souls may worship Me, yet in My absolute wholeness, I recognise no division or distinctions.

Awareness is a partless whole. It cannot be objectified and it cannot be divided into "this" and "that". It's impossible to divorce anything from Awareness, because it is the eternal and ever-present basis of Reality. As *satya*, the causeless Cause behind the world of phenomenal effect (which we call *mithya*), Awareness cannot be separate from the world of objects any more than a gold bracelet can be separate from the gold. Mithya depends upon satya for its existence just as the bracelet depends upon the gold and the pot upon the clay. Ultimately, when name and form are negated as but an incidental characteristic, we find no difference between the two. The Self alone is.

7. Neither ignorance nor doubt cause the slightest ripple in Me. The activities of the mind, and all its thoughts and impulses, are merely bubbles rising and dissolving on the surface of a lake.

Freedom is freedom irrespective of whatever happens to the body and mind, both of which function according to their respective natures. No matter what ripples appear upon the lake of the mind, the Self is ever free and untouched by anything in the maya world—whether externally, in terms of one's circumstances and environment, or internally, as the functioning of one's body and mind.

8. By My nature, I pervade and lend existence to all the subtle and gross elements. I alone grant softness to the soft, hardness to the hard, sweetness to the sweet, and bitterness to the bitter.

9. As water cannot be perceived independently of its qualities of clearness, fluidity, and softness, the realm of matter (prakriti) cannot be perceived independently of the spirit (purusha) which reveals and enlivens it.

Prakriti and purusha are concepts discussed in greater depth in the Bhagavad Gita. To recapitulate, prakriti refers to the phenomenal world of gross and subtle matter (maya), while purusha refers to the universal and all-pervading Awareness (the Self) which grants it life much as the sun illumines the moon with its reflected light. Whatever life and sentience the world of matter enjoys is granted only by the enlivening principle of Awareness.

10. Uncategorised by name or by speech, subtler than the subtlest, and beyond the reach of the mind, intellect or senses, is the stainless Lord of the universe.

This Lord of the universe refers to the Self; the subtlest of the subtle; that which pervades all things as their innermost Existence/Essence, but which can never be captured or objectified by the material senses. The job of the senses is to connect with their respective sense objects in the world of the form. The Self, although unavailable to the senses, is That which illumines them, much as electricity grants life to a lightbulb.

11. Upon knowing the limitless Self, how can the limited ego self remain? How can there be a "you", and how can there be a world?

Because the senses perceive a world of duality, the mind takes itself to be part of that multiplicity; one discrete form amid uncountable billions of forms. If the Self is limitless, however, then how can a limited ego remain? Vedanta reveals this notion of a separate self to be a fabrication of the mind; a superimposition rooted in ignorance of the true nature of reality.

The source of our suffering is our tendency to take appearance to be real by confusing the apparent with the actual. Because the Self is, in essence, formless and without division, all appearance of form and division is a product of maya; of appearance alone.

12. The Self is described as being like the sky. Its nature is pure unalloyed Awareness, without defect, ever perfect and whole.

13. This Awareness does not move about the earth, nor does It dwell in fire. It cannot be blown by the wind, nor covered by water. Though It takes all forms, It remains formless.

14. Despite pervading all of space and time, nothing pervades the Self. Both within and without, It is indivisible and limitless.

15. Although the subtlest of the subtle, beyond perception, without attribute and unavailable to the senses, the Self of which the great Sages speak can be realised as That which underlies all temporary states of mind.

The Vedantic scriptures describe the Self as the *adhistanam*, which means the foundation, basis or support of the entire creation. It underlies everything as the very essence and, indeed, the substance of all things; at once both transcendent and immanent.

Yoga has superb practical application and is employed by Vedanta as a means of preparing the mind for Knowledge, much as a field is cultivated prior to planting. However, yogic philosophy can cause confusion when it comes to enlightenment, for the yoga sutras purport enlightenment to be a state of mind called *chitta vritti narodah,* or the cessation of all thought.

Moksha, however, is not about the eradication of thought or the cultivation of certain states of mind. After all, if freedom depends upon the mind being a certain way then it's not freedom at all—because the mind is, by its very nature, ever shifting according to the play of the *gunas* (qualities of gross and subtle matter).

For freedom to be true freedom, it must be unqualified and independent of extraneous factors. True freedom is realising that, as the Self, you are always and ever free, in spite of all external variables, including the condition of the body and the state of the mind; such states being, as this verse states, temporary by nature.

This freedom doesn't depend upon the mind being *sattvic*, tranquil and serene. That certainly helps, and is key to helping assimilate this knowledge. But even if the mind is subject to agitation (*rajas*) or dullness (*tamas*), the Self, which is the Awareness in which the mind has its Source, is ever unaffected and, therefore, forever free.

16. Practising constant discrimination and detachment from objects of perception, the ardent seeker of liberation is eventually freed from bondage to the material world by realising their non-separation from the Absolute.

Discrimination and detachment are the two primary qualifications necessary for Self-knowledge to liberate the mind. Discrimination means the ability to separate the real from the apparently real; the eternal from the fleeting, and truth from ignorance. It also means being clear about your true goal: liberation through the rigorous application of Self-knowledge to the mind.

Detachment from sense objects is also necessary, because until you cultivate a high degree of dispassion your mind will continually fixate upon the world of objects. As a result, you'll find your attention devoured by ceaseless desires, aversions and intractable attachment to sense pleasures.

Only when you're completely clear that nothing in the world of form can bring you lasting happiness and fulfilment will you devote the necessary time and effort to following the teaching of Vedanta and applying it to the mind.

17. For the deadly poison of worldly lust, which so deludes the mind, there is but one antidote: To reclaim your nature as the desireless and ever whole Self.

The basis of samsara is the erroneous sense of being a limited, lacking being — who, in order to extract some happiness from the world, must struggle to get the world to conform to our likes and dislikes. The problem is, the more we act out of our desires and fears, the greater this strengthens our psychological conditioning, further cementing the sense of being a finite ego/doer/enjoyer.

There is no end to desire. Just as a fire will never concede that it's burned enough, desire is an inferno that can never be satiated. Desire itself is suffering. After all, when we satisfy our desires we feel good precisely because, for a brief moment, we are free of desire. The only way out of this is Self-Knowledge: specifically, the realisation that, as the Self, we are already whole and complete.

The ego's sense of self-lack was based on ignorance alone. The solution to ignorance can only be knowledge, and the king of knowledge, *raja vidya*, is Self-Knowledge. Knowing our very nature to be Wholeness itself destroys desire by eradicating it at its very root; shattering the misapprehension of ourselves as a limited and incomplete entity.

18. The world of objects is seen without, and the world of thoughts is perceived within. That which allows all to be experienced, yet which transcends all experience, is the Eternal Self.

This false duality, the sense of being a separate entity living in a disconnected external world, is negated by realising the Self as the sole Reality.

Both the jiva's inner and outer world; the subjective world of thought and imagination and the objective world of forms and objects are experienced in Awareness. Awareness unites the two and cannot be separated from experience at any time.

As the causeless Cause of the creation, the Self is that from which all form and experience arises and that by which it is experienced. It's the one thing that can never be discounted or negated, for it is the ever-present and unchanging substratum of existence.

19. What we experience outwardly as the world of form is born of prakriti. Pervading prakriti, like the milk within a coconut, is the inner Source of life.

20. If the outer world is akin to the husk of a coconut, the pulp is prakriti, and the sweet milk concealed within is the Self.

Again, prakriti is a term to describe the material aspect of creation at this, the empirical order of reality. While ultimately only the formless, limitless Self exists, at this level of reality the mind and senses do experience a discrete world of form and differentiation.

For beginner and intermediate students, Vedanta uses the concepts of prakriti and purusha, thereby admitting a provisional, apparent duality. The material level of prakriti, itself inert and insentient, depends upon purusha, the principle of universal Consciousness or Awareness, to grant it life, much as the lightbulb requires the presence of electricity in order to shine. Contrary to what materialists assume, this purusha (the Self), can exist without prakriti (matter), but prakriti cannot exist without purusha.

Purusha is the independent Cause from which the creation arises and into which it resolves. The material universe, therefore, can no more exist without the Self, Consciousness, than a bracelet can exist without the gold it is made of. Indeed, what we call "bracelet" is merely the gold configured into a specific name and form.

Similarly, the phenomenal reality is nothing but Consciousness "appearing" as certain names and forms. Neither the bracelet nor the phenomenal world possess an independent existence of their own. As mithya (unreal), both borrow their limited, time-bound existence from their underlying Cause, which is satya (real).

21. As on a clear full moon night when the moon is seen as one, so do the wise see only one Self in all. The sense of duality is a product of distorted vision.

Like the weary traveller at dusk mistaking the rope for a snake—which is to say, superimposing an imaginary "snake" onto the rope—the unenlightened mistake the myriad forms of maya as real, thus superimposing duality upon the non-dual Self. Both are cases of distorted vision.

22. Duality can never pertain to the Self, for universal Being is all-pervading. Those who teach this Truth are great souls, worthy of endless gratitude.

As we already established, the word guru means "dispeller of darkness". Darkness is a metaphor for ignorance; "to be in the dark". Because this ignorance is the source of all our existential sorrow, it is only natural to have eternal gratitude to the one who removes this ignorance and its concomitant sorrow.

23. By the grace of a guru, both the wise and the ignorant may attain Self-Knowledge, but only those who cross the ocean of worldly attachment will actualise this knowledge.

As stated before, Vedanta works in three stages. The first stage, shravana, means "hearing". You must first simply expose your mind to the teaching by listening to the words of the teacher with an open mind free of preconceived notions. The key is not to try to evaluate the teaching by comparing it to what you think you already know, because much of what you think you know is actually ignorance masquerading as truth. This stands to reason, because if you already knew the Truth, you'd be free of suffering and would have no need of Vedanta in the first place. So this stage requires a receptive and inquiring mind.

The second stage, manana, is where you apply reason in order to fully grasp what you've been taught. It means working through any doubts and confusion as they arise, with the help of the teacher. Although an element of faith is necessary in order to trust the teacher and commit to attaining the knowledge, this is not a blind faith. It's no good simply accepting what you've been taught without properly understanding the teaching. It has to make perfect sense or else it will be little more than an empty doctrine; just another belief system. At this stage, the Knowledge must be converted to understanding.

The final stage of Vedanta is called nididhyasana, and this means continuously contemplating and integrating the Knowledge until it becomes fully assimilated; which is, to say, until it becomes the mind's new operating system. If the first stage provides knowledge, the second converts it to understanding, and the third and final stage converts understanding to conviction.

As this verse states, both the wise and the ignorant can attain Knowledge of the Self, but this knowledge will only bear fruit when it is fully internalised by the mind. To return to our computer metaphor, you can download new software for your computer but nothing will happen until you install and run it.

Dattatreya states here that one of the keys to assimilating this Knowledge is to "cross the ocean of worldly attachment", which means developing detachment from the world of sense objects. Only then will the mind gain the necessary objectivity and discrimination to catalyse Self-Knowledge into liberation.

24. Those who are free from binding desire and aversion, who are devoted to the good of all beings, and whose Knowledge is firm and mind steady will attain liberation.

Vedanta makes it clear that when it comes to liberation, success or failure is determined by the presence of absence of the mental qualifications specified by Shankara: specifically, discrimination, dispassion, discipline of the mind and senses, the ability to focus the mind, faith in the teaching and the teacher, and desire for liberation. Just as seeds will only grow in an appropriately fertile field, so will Self-Knowledge only take root in a suitably prepared mind.

25. As the space inside a jar merges into the outside space when the jar is broken, so do the Self-Realised, upon the shedding of the body, merge with Universal Consciousness.

This "merging" is, in fact, simply the realisation that you were never separate from or other than the Consciousness/Awareness that is the Self.

26. It is said that the future trajectory of the soul is determined by one's last thought at the time of death, but those established in Self-Knowledge are not bound by thought.

27. One may talk about the destiny of those worldly souls who are bound by action, but the destiny of those established in Self-Knowledge cannot be spoken, for it transcends words.

Those who know themselves to be the Self are bound by neither thought, word, or deed. They abide in Awareness as Awareness and, having negated the ego's sense of doership and ownership and neutralised the mind's binding desires and aversions, are no longer bound by samsara's cycle of birth and death.

28. The enlightened one has no particular path. He or she simply renounces duality by ceasing to imagine things. For them, liberation is easily attained.

All experience is the product of consciousness plus thought. Consciousness is constant and eternal, whereas thought changes moment by moment. Duality is actually caused by thought; by the mind's tendency to create division and differentiation, and to carve up reality into "this" and "that"; "me" and "you"; "good" and "bad". We then inhabit an entirely subjective world of duality. As Dattatreya elegantly states, the liberated overcome duality "by ceasing to imagine things." They are no longer identified with thought or its contents, but with the underlying, eternal, Non-dual (yet ordinary and everyday) Consciousness that illumines all thought.

29. When the enlightened die, whether in a sacred or profane place, they never need enter a mother's womb again, for they, in essence, merge into Brahman [the Self].

By realising one's essential identity as Brahman, the Self, and fully assimilating this knowledge, the jiva's individual "karmic account" is deleted, so to speak. No longer pushed and pulled by binding desires and fears, there is nothing to compel them to keep assuming new bodies in order to scratch those karmic itches. No longer falsely identifying themselves as a limited body and mind subject to a false sense of doership and authorship, they abide in Awareness as Awareness.

30. Those who fully realise the innate, birthless and eternal nature of the Self never become tainted even while enjoying the fruits of desire. Ever free of stain, such souls are no longer chained by karma. Those who have mastered the mind and senses, and who fix their mind on the Self, are never bound.

For the liberated, this entire play of maya—the appearance of form and differentiation within the formless and undifferentiated Self—is seen as *Ishvara*, or God (the technical term is *Saguna Brahman*, meaning the Self with form and attribute). All karma belongs to Ishvara, including the fruits of past actions. By knowing oneself to be, as pure Consciousness/Awareness, free of all action, the liberated soul is unbound even as the body, mind and senses continue engaging with the world and reaping the results of past actions and desires, both good and bad.

31. The liberated are beyond maya, beyond comparison, beyond form, beyond all supports, beyond the body and its sustenance, beyond duality, delusion, and power. It is the Self, the Supreme Eternal, that such a soul attains.

32. The attainment of the liberated soul is not the Highest Knowledge, nor initiation, nor the clean-shaven head of the renunciate. It is not a guru, nor disciples, nor worldly treasure, nor is it the practice of yogic postures or the wearing of ceremonial adornment. It is the Self, the Supreme Eternal, that they attain.

The liberated require no spiritual badges of office. Those who feel they need to somehow display their attainment—to make a show of "being enlightened"—are most likely still identified with the ego and its in-built sense of limitation and smallness. Those who truly know themselves to be free need no outward validation.

33. The liberated soul envisions neither Shiva nor Shakti, nor any other gods. Kundalini and other forces do not pertain to them, nor the feet of the Lord. They do not perceive the soul as being like the contents of a glass jar. It is the Self, the Supreme Eternal, that they attain.

The liberated know the entire phenomenal world, both gross and subtle, to be mithya. Like a wave on the ocean, mithya enjoys an apparent existence, but because it depends entirely upon its cause for its existence, as the wave depends upon the ocean, it has no inherent reality of its own. Only the Self, the independent Cause and totality of Existence, has any reality (satya). All else, including the highest spiritual states and dimensions, is mithya alone.

34. They attain the Essence from which the universe of sentient and insentient forms is born; That in which it abides and That to which it returns like waves on the ocean. It is the Self, the Supreme Eternal, that they attain.

35. The attainment of the enlightened is not control of the breath, nor fixed gazing or yogic postures. Neither knowledge or ignorance pertain to them, nor purification of the nerve-currents. It is the Self, the Supreme Eternal, that they attain.

This verse makes the point that spiritual practice, in this case yoga, is not an end in itself, but a means to prepare the mind and nothing more. The real attainment, insomuch as it can be called an attainment, is the assimilated Knowledge of one's true nature as the Self.

36. This attainment is not of something external or separate from oneself. It is, indeed, beyond both objectification and comparison. It is the Self, the Supreme Eternal, that they attain.

The Self cannot be objectified because it is subtler than the mind, senses and intellect. As the very light of Awareness, it is not an object, but the Eternal Subject.

37. It matters not whether they have perfect concentration and control of the senses, or whether they take action or refrain from action. It is the Self, the Supreme Eternal, that they attain.

While preparation of the mind is essential to facilitate the full assimilation of Self-knowledge, liberation, by its very definition, must be unqualified. If liberation is dependent upon the mind, body and senses being in a certain state, as yogis believe, then it is not liberation, because the moment the mind, body and senses shift out of that coveted state, the "liberation" will be lost.

Liberation must necessarily be independent of all factors. The enlightened, being steady in the Knowledge of their nature as Awareness, are free regardless of the condition or quality of the body and mind. Whether thoughts are present or absent in the mind, the liberated are unmoved, for the Self is unbound by thought. Action may or may not take place, yet, knowing themselves to be the Awareness in which action takes place, the liberated are also unbound by action.

38. It is beyond the mind, intellect, body and sense organs; beyond the subtle elements and the five gross elements; beyond the ego-sense and beyond even space. It is the Self, the Supreme Eternal, that they attain.

39. Abiding as the Eternal Self, the liberated soul is free from all dictates, with a mind devoid of duality. Neither purity nor impurity, nor distinguishing attributes, nor fortune or misfortune pertain to such a soul. It is the Self, the Supreme Eternal, that they attain.

Although the mind and senses still register the maya world as before, the liberated soul knows that duality is just a superimposition upon non-duality; which is to say, an appearance in Awareness.

40. If the Self is subtler than the mind and speech, how can the words of a guru capture it? How can the words of any teaching reveal that which is the essence of Existence and which is ever-shining and self-illumining?

Because it is subtler than the subtlest and unobjectifiable by any means, Vedanta reveals the Self not by adding knowledge of the Self as such (besides, we actually already have knowledge of the Self because we all know that we exist and are conscious), but by removing the ignorance we have about the nature of that self. The Self is self-shining and self-revealing. Like the sun, it needs no other source of light to reveal it. The best the guru can do is to remove the erroneous notions we have about who we are and, through a process of sustained self-inquiry, strip away the idea that appearance is real, and that we are simply an assemblage of body, mind and ego. When the false is negated, what remains is the Truth.

Chapter 3

1. How shall I worship the Eternal Self which is devoid of the qualities constituting the material universe? Beyond both attachment and non-attachment, formless and yet the substance of all forms, having no attribute and yet that which enables all attributes, Shiva is the eternal, all-pervading totality.

The subtlest of the subtle, the Self, here referred to as Shiva, is that which underlies and pervades all forms and objects as their innermost essence; at once both immanent and transcendent. It is the sum total of all that exists—the very essence of Existence itself; that which lends existence to the world of form much as the ocean lends existence to the rolling waves upon its surface.

2. Shiva, the Eternal Self, has no colour, whether white or yellow, and is at once both the cause and effect. Beyond all doubt, I know that I am Shiva, the Universal Consciousness. Tell me, my friend, how can I bow down to my own Self?

Whereas the first verse provides Indirect Knowledge (knowledge of the Self as an object), this second verse converts that Knowledge to Direct Knowledge by affirming that the Self not only exists, but that *I am* that Self. Indirect Knowledge is the necessary first step, but without Direct Knowledge—without knowing that we *are* pure Consciousness or Awareness; the One without a second—we will never taste the fruits of liberation.

3. Neither with root nor rootless, I am like a sun eternally shining. Neither hidden nor unhidden, I am like a sun eternally shining. Neither illumined or unillumined, I am like a sun eternally shining. I am the liberating nectar of Self-Knowledge; I am all-pervading like the sky.

The nature of the Self may seem paradoxical to the mind; being neither "this" nor "that", but the sum total and inherent essence of all things. Light is an apt metaphor; the Self being a beginningless, endless and causeless Light forever shining; one which reveals and enlivens all form and experience. The final sentence in this verse is a refrain repeated throughout the rest of this chapter; an exhortation that, as the Self, we are endless and all-pervading like the vast and boundless sky.

4. How can desirelessness or desire pertain to me? How can I possess either non-attachment or attachment? How can I speak of either formlessness or form? I am the liberating nectar of Self-Knowledge; I am all-pervading like the sky.

5. How can I speak of non-duality, when it encompasses the world of apparent duality? How can I speak of the

whole, when it contains all seeming division? How can I speak of the eternal, when within it exists the non-eternal? I am the liberating nectar of Self-Knowledge; I am all-pervading like the sky.

6. My nature is neither gross nor subtle. I neither come nor go. I am without beginning, middle or end. I am neither large nor small. With my words I share the secrets of the true nature of Reality. I am the liberating nectar of Self-Knowledge; I am all-pervading like the sky.

Through a process of negation, these verses reveal our true nature to be independent of the world of ephemeral forms and beyond all division and duality. The Upanishads offer many seemingly contradictory statements about the Self, proclaiming it to be at once greater than the greatest of all things imaginable and yet "smaller than a mustard seed". These words reveal the Self to be neither contained nor constrained by the phenomenal world. As the substratum and support of the universe, It pervades the universe both within and without. Subtler than the mind and senses, it cannot be directly apprehended, but is that by which apprehension is made possible. Indeed, the Kena Upanishad declares the Self to be "the eye of the eye, the ear of the ear and the mind of the mind" — in other words, the Intelligence and Sentience that reveals all sight, all sound, all thought, perception and experience. It cannot be contained, for it is, as these verses repeatedly state, "all-pervading like the sky".

7. Know that the sense organs are as insubstantial as space. Know that the sense objects are also as insubstantial as space. Know that, as the Self, the Eternal One, I am taintless and neither bound nor free. I am the liberating nectar of Self-Knowledge; I am all-pervading like the sky.

Vedantic inquiry negates anything objectifiable by the mind and senses as being mithya, or only apparently real. Like a mirage appearing in the mind of the thirsty desert traveller, mithya is an appearance in Awareness that relies upon Awareness for its borrowed and temporary existence. Modern physics verifies Dattatreya's words of millennia ago by revealing physical matter to be, at the subatomic level, as "insubstantial as space". Unfortunately, the physical sciences have no way to understand the Eternal Self; the boundless Awareness in which the universe arises like the desert mirage. For that, we must rely upon the Upanishads and the elucidations of sages such as Dattatreya.

8. I am beyond the intellect and imperceptible as an object of cognition. Although I am not hidden, the mind cannot reach me. I am beyond the senses and imperceptible as an object of perception. Although I am not hidden, the senses cannot reach me. I am the liberating nectar of Self-Knowledge; I am all-pervading like the sky.

Seek the Self and you will never find it, for it is always the subject and never the object. Again, it bears repeating that the mind cannot perceive that which is subtler than it—and, indeed, of a different order of reality. What hope does the dreamer have of perceiving the waker? And yet, although the two inhabit different orders of reality (the dream state and the waking state respectively) the two are not separate, for they both belong to the one and same Consciousness.

9. Free of karma, I am the fire that burns all karmas. Free of sorrow, I am the fire that removes all sorrow. Free of form, I am the fire that releases all forms. I am the liberating nectar of Self-Knowledge; I am all-pervading like the sky.

Self-Knowledge is the fire that burns away karma and sorrow by neutralising the ego's erroneous sense of doership and ownership. Freedom from form is the Knowledge that, as the Self, you are beyond form. You are the light by which all objects, actions and experiences are witnessed; ever shining, ever the same, and, thus, ever free.

10. Free of sin, I am the fire that burns all sins. Free of prescribed duty, I am the fire that purifies all duties. Unbound, I am the fire that breaks all bondage. I am the liberating nectar of Self-Knowledge; I am all-pervading like the sky.

11. I am beyond both existence and non-existence; neither pertain to me. I am beyond both union and separation; neither pertain to me. I am beyond both thought and the absence of thought; neither pertain to me. I am the liberating nectar of Self-Knowledge; I am all-pervading like the sky.

The question of duality and Non-duality never arises for the Self, which, as the unbroken totality of Existence itself, simply *is*. In spite of all appearances to the contrary (courtesy of maya), there is nothing other than it, rendering any notions of duality and differentiation inapplicable. The following verses highlight this by emphasising that, as the Absolute, the Self remains untouched and unaffected by anything in the world of form, including the very qualities that comprise it (ie., the *gunas*).

12. I am unswayed by either delusion or non-delusion; neither such thought affects me. I am unswayed by either happiness or sorrow; neither such thought affects me. I am unswayed by either desire or desirelessness; neither such thought affects me. I am the liberating nectar of Self-Knowledge; I am all-pervading like the sky.

13. The creeping vine of samsara does not affect me at all. Even the greatest pleasure and contentment does not affect me at all. Ignorance and worldly bondage does not affect me at all. I am the liberating nectar of Self-Knowledge; I am all-pervading like the sky.

14. The suffering of agitation caused by rajo-guna does not affect me at all. The lethargy and grief caused by tamo-guna does not affect me at all. The pleasure of righteousness caused by sattva-guna does not affect me at all. I am the liberating nectar of Self-Knowledge; I am all-pervading like the sky.

15. Neither grief, sorrows nor pleasures have any affect on Me, for I am other than the intellect. None of the difficulties inherent in the pursuit of yoga have any affect on Me, for I am other than the mind. None of the challenges life presents have any affect on Me, for I am other than the ego. I am the liberating nectar of Self-Knowledge; I am all-pervading like the sky.

16. In Me, both decision and indecision resolve, for I am beyond thought. In Me, both dreaming and waking resolve, for I neither sleep nor wake. In Me, both the animate and inanimate resolve, for I am neither in motion or motionless. I am the liberating nectar of Self-Knowledge; I am all-pervading like the sky.

17. I am not the knower, the known, nor the instrument of knowledge. I am beyond the reach of words, mind and intellect, for how can the One Reality ever be described by words? I am the liberating nectar of Self-Knowledge; I am all-pervading like the sky.

18. I am neither divided nor undivided, for I am the One Reality. I am neither within nor without, for I am the One Reality. I was never created, therefore I have no substance of creation. I am the liberating nectar of Self-Knowledge; I am all-pervading like the sky.

19. I am free of the grief of attachment, for I am the One Reality. I am free of the sorrows of fate, for I am the One Reality. I am free of the pain of worldly existence, for I am the One Reality. I am the liberating nectar of Self-Knowledge; I am all-pervading like the sky.

These and subsequent verses are excellent koans for meditation and deep contemplation. Through a process sometimes called *neti neti* ("not this, not this"), they aim to strip away all sense of limitation and duality, revealing the pure and stainless Self to be that which is One without a second; utterly undivided in any way, subtler than the grasp of the mind and intellect—and uncreated, thus not subject to the laws of creation.

20. Since I am beyond the three states of consciousness, how could I be the fourth? Since I am beyond the three types of time, how could I be the fourth? I am the eternal abode of serenity; the absolute Reality. I am the liberating nectar of Self-Knowledge; I am all-pervading like the sky.

This verse refutes the common misunderstanding that the Self is what we call *turiya*, or the "fourth" state of consciousness (the other three being the waking, dreaming and deep sleep states). The dictionary defines "state" as a "mode, or condition of mind and temperament". Such states are by definition variable, changeable and dependent upon external factors. Clearly the Self cannot therefore be defined as a "state". Even the often-used term "natural state" is problematic. The Self is the causeless Cause by which all states exist, while Itself unaffected by any such conditions.

21. Descriptions such as "long" or "short" do not pertain to Me, nor do the terms "broad" or "narrow", "angular" or "circular". I am the liberating nectar of Self-Knowledge; I am all-pervading like the sky.

22. I have neither mother or father, nor son or daughter. I was never born, nor shall I ever die. I am without mind. Unwavering and steady, I am the absolute Reality. I am the liberating nectar of Self-Knowledge; I am all-pervading like the sky.

23. I am, by nature, boundless and beyond such distinctions as pure and impure. I am, by nature, boundless and beyond such distinctions as attachment and non-attachment. I am, by nature, boundless and beyond such distinctions as divided and undivided. I am the liberating nectar of Self-Knowledge; I am all-pervading like the sky.

24. As the supreme Reality, I am stainless and non-dual; how can Brahma and all the gods and beings of heaven have their place in Me? I am the liberating nectar of Self-Knowledge; I am all-pervading like the sky.

25. How shall I, the taintless One, speak when I am both "this" and "not this"? How shall I, the taintless One, speak when I am the unsupported support of all? How shall I, the taintless One, speak when I am both attribute and attribute-less? I am the liberating nectar of Self-Knowledge; I am all-pervading like the sky.

26. I am the Supreme; beyond both action and actionlessness. I am the greatest bliss; beyond both attachment and non-attachment. I am the everlasting bliss; beyond both form and formlessness. I am the liberating nectar of Self-Knowledge; I am all-pervading like the sky.

27. This dreamworld of maya affects me not. The deceitfulness and arrogance of man affects me not. The truth or falsehood of speech affects me not. I am the liberating nectar of Self-Knowledge; I am all-pervading like the sky.

As the Self, this waking world of transient forms and experiences affects you no more than the world of your dreams at night. As the Self, you pervade and sustain the relative world of form, both gross and subtle, but remain unaffected by its dreamlike kaleidoscope of modifications.

28. I have neither night nor day, for I am subject to no duality. I never awaken, for I was never not awake. I need not strive for purity, for I am unaffected by thought or mood. I am the liberating nectar of Self-Knowledge; I am all-pervading like the sky.

The term "awakening" has become synonymous with "enlightenment" in modern spiritual circles. But, as Dattatreya reveals here, the Self is never not awake. "Awakening", therefore, can only apply to the mind, and since enlightenment is the knowledge that you are not the mind, this immediately renders the term invalid.

29. Neither am I the Lord, nor am I not the Lord, for I am the formless Self. I transcend both the presence and absence of mind, for I am the formless Self. I am the liberating nectar of Self-Knowledge; I am all-pervading like the sky.

30. I am the abode of forest and temple; what more can I say? I do nothing, yet by Me everything is done; what more can I say? I ever abide in the equilibrium of evenness, for I am the formless Self. I am the liberating nectar of Self-Knowledge; I am all-pervading like the sky.

31. I am neither jiva [individual] nor am I not jiva; I endlessly shine. I am neither the seed nor am I not the seed; I endlessly shine. I am neither liberation nor am I bondage; I endlessly shine. I am the liberating nectar of Self-Knowledge; I am all-pervading like the sky.

32. I am without beginning or birth; I endlessly shine. I am unaffected by the worldly sorrow of samsara; I endlessly shine. I am unaffected by death; I endlessly shine. I am the liberating nectar of Self-Knowledge; I am all-pervading like the sky.

33. Although You may be spoken of, You have neither name nor form. Whether divided or undivided, You are all that is. Why then, O mind, do you shamelessly grieve? I am the liberating nectar of Self-Knowledge; I am all-pervading like the sky.

Verse thirty-three sees a shift of perspective. Dattrateya moves from speaking of himself from the perspective of the Self to addressing the listener as the Self. That is the difference between Indirect Knowledge and Direct Knowledge. The conflict here is between the mind's "shameless grief" which, being the product of Self-ignorance, is quite at odds with our true nature as the eternal and untouchable shining Self. The next few verses develop this theme, aiming to strip away worldly sorrow by revealing it to be an illegitimate sorrow based on self-misidentification.

CHAPTER THREE

34. Why do you weep and fret, my friend? There is no old age or death for you. Why do you weep and fret, my friend? There is no pain of birth for you. Why do you weep and fret, my friend? You are untouchable by anything in this world. I am the liberating nectar of Self-Knowledge; I am all-pervading like the sky.

35. Why do you weep and fret, my friend? You have no natural form. Why do you weep and fret, my friend? You are not subject to limitation or deformity. Why do you weep and fret, my friend? You can never grow old. I am the liberating nectar of Self-Knowledge; I am all-pervading like the sky.

36. Why do you weep and fret, my friend? You are not subject to ageing. Why do you weep and fret, my friend? You are not subject to mind and thought. Why do you weep and fret, my friend? You beyond the senses. I am the liberating nectar of Self-Knowledge; I am all-pervading like the sky.

37. Why do you weep and fret, my friend? You are impervious to lust. Why do you weep and fret, my friend? You are untouched by greed. Why do you weep and fret, my friend? You are unmoved by infatuation. I am the liberating nectar of Self-Knowledge; I am all-pervading like the sky.

38. Why spend your life chasing wealth? You have no property to your name. Why spend your life chasing wealth? You have no spouse to feed. Why spend your life chasing wealth? Nothing here belongs to you. I am the liberating nectar of Self-Knowledge; I am all-pervading like the sky.

39. Neither you nor I are attached to this world of ephemeral forms. It is only the shameless mind that divides the One into a realm of false duality. You and I are beyond both division and non-division. I am the liberating nectar of Self-Knowledge; I am all-pervading like the sky.

40. In essence, your nature has not the slightest dispassion. Nor, in essence, does it have even the slightest attachment or desire. I am the liberating nectar of Self-Knowledge; I am all-pervading like the sky.

41. Your nature is free of all objects, whether the mind is absorbed in deep meditation or directed to the world of external forms. There is nothing outside of you, for you are beyond both space and time. I am the liberating nectar of Self-Knowledge; I am all-pervading like the sky.

42. I have shared with you the Highest Truth; there is no "you", no "me", no teacher or student. The Supreme Reality is both self-existent, self-evident and ever shining. I am the liberating nectar of Self-Knowledge; I am all-pervading like the sky.

The Highest Truth is one of non-division. Everything is the one, immortal, undivided Self; the one Awareness in which all seeming form and differentiation is experienced. Self-existent, self-evident and ever shining, it needs nothing to illumine it. It is an all-pervading light, without a source and without beginning or end.

43. As the Supreme Reality, how could my nature be of bliss? As the Supreme Reality, how could my nature be devoid of bliss? As the Supreme Reality, how does either knowledge or ignorance pertain to me? As the Supreme Reality, I am One–existing everywhere like space.

44. Knowing It to be neither fire nor air, Realise the One! Knowing It to be neither earth nor water, Realise the One! Knowing that It neither comes nor goes, Realise the One! Knowing that, like space, It pervades all, Realise the One!

45. My nature is neither emptiness nor fullness. My nature is neither pure nor impure. My nature is neither form nor formlessness. My nature is unfathomable, for I am the Supreme Reality!

We often assign words to describe the Self, such as bliss or fullness, but ultimately it must be understood that the Self is beyond description, beyond label and categorisation, and thoroughly devoid of duality of any kind. It can only be known as That which knows; as the Sentience illumining the instruments of body and mind.

46. Renounce, renounce the world of attachment and suffering. Then renounce the renouncing as well. Enjoy the nectar of your true Self; pure, immortal and free.

A certain degree of effort is required to tame the mind and render it a fit receptacle for Self-Knowledge. Yet, because effort tends to reinforce the sense of doership, there comes a time when even that should be abandoned. This renunciation of which Dattatreya speaks, however, isn't so much the renunciation of action itself (because, let's face it, there's never a time when action isn't required in life). It is the renunciation of the notion of doership; of being an author and agent of action. The Bhagavad Gita unfolds the specifics of this teaching in great depth throughout its eighteen chapters.

Chapter 4

1. Nothing can be added to or taken away from pure Awareness or Consciousness. So why practise offerings and prostrations? Why perform worship with flowers and leaves? Why engage in meditation and the repetition of mantra? The worshipper and the object of worship are, in fact, one.

One of the greatest controversies in the realm of modern spirituality, and particularly in the sphere of Non-duality, is the issue of spiritual practice. To practice or not to practice? That is the question! Many modern teachers dismiss spiritual practice as an unnecessary indulgence, declaring that "you are already free". However, while this might be true from the perspective of the Self (the Self, after all, is limitless and thus impervious to bondage), it's unlikely to be the case for the poor suffering jiva.

Herein lies the seeming contradiction at the heart of Vedantic teaching: there is nothing you can do to become free because you are already free. You cannot *become* the Self because you are already the Self. What else could you be? The problem is ignorance alone. This ignorance exists in the mind as faulty patterns of thought and self-misconception.

Vedanta remedies this self-ignorance like nothing else; stripping away the notion that you are a limited body/mind/ego, and revealing your true nature to the field of Awareness or Consciousness in which they appear. The problem is Vedanta comes with a set of stipulations. It requires a mature and qualified mind in order to work: specifically, a stable, peaceful, discriminating and dispassionate mind capable of withdrawing from worldly attachments and focusing on the teaching for sustained periods of time. Binding *vasanas* (conditioned impressions and tendencies) must be rendered non-binding and the mind's entrenched likes and dislikes sufficiently neutralised. This isn't something that will happen on its own. Such a mind must be consciously cultivated through the steadfast application of karma yoga, meditation and devotion. This requires much in the way of discipline, perseverance and diligence.

As stated in the introduction, the Avadhuta Gita is not a beginner's text. Dattatreya's words here apply to those whose minds are already highly pure and sattvic, for only such a mind will grasp and actualise the teachings of the scriptures. For those whose minds are liberated by the light of Self-Knowledge and who are resolute in the realisation that they are pure Awareness, there is no further need to engage in spiritual practice. This doesn't, however, mean that they won't perform spiritual practice, because what better way to spend one's life than worshipping the divine beneficence of God? But they do so with the clear understanding that no separation exists between the devotee and the object of devotion.

2. The Universal Consciousness I am remains free of bondage and liberation; free of purity and impurity; and free of union and separation. I, myself, am the essence of Freedom; I pervade everything like space.

The qualities of duality pertain only to mithya; to the world of objects, form and experience. As the Self, the one, Non-dual Consciousness, we exist free of all duality. This knowledge, which Vedanta calls *raja vidya*, the "king of knowledge", is the jiva's ticket to freedom.

3. Philosophers and spiritual aspirants endlessly debate the reality or unreality of the phenomenal world, but such concepts have no meaning to me. Freedom is My nature; maya does not pertain to Me.

4. I have no fault, nor am I faultless. I have no beginning, nor am I beginningless. I have neither division nor lack of division. Freedom is My nature; maya does not pertain to Me.

This and subsequent verses are declarations from the perspective of the Self. Again, they highlight that the opposites of duality pertain only to maya, the apparent world, and not to the pure Awareness pervading, underlying and transcending it. These are exultations of freedom; the song of the Avadhuta, or liberated soul.

5. As the undivided Self, neither ignorance or knowledge exist in Me. How can I thus speak of knowing or not knowing? Freedom is My nature; maya does not pertain to Me.

6. Neither righteousness or sin exist in Me, nor bondage or liberation. I cannot be described as either united or separated. Freedom is My nature; maya does not pertain to Me.

7. "Better" or "worse" are meaningless concepts to Me. I have neither friend or enemy. How then can I speak of "good" and "evil"? Freedom is My nature; maya does not pertain to Me.

Some people, out of misunderstanding, criticise Vedanta for adopting what they assume is a position of moral relativism. "If everything is the Self and there is no good or bad," they say, "then what's to stop people from raping and pillaging their way through life?" It's important to understand that at the Absolute order of reality there is no division, no duality, no opposites and, therefore, no "good" or "bad". The Self, being the totality of all that is, exists beyond such concepts.

Within the realm of maya, however, good and bad clearly exist, as determined by the law of dharma. "Good" might be defined as that which adheres to and supports dharma, while "bad" can be defined as anything that contravenes dharma, causing unnecessary suffering. There's no escaping dharma, for it is a natural law built into the very fabric of the creation. All beings must conform to dharma and the failure to do so invariably results in pain and suffering.

Again, Dattatreya is speaking here not from the level of the jiva in the relative world, but from the perspective of the Self. You can be sure, however, that Self-Realised beings automatically follow dharma with impeccable resolve. After all, having surmounted the ego and its entrenched desires and attachments, they have no reason to violate it. They are automatically "good" because they live in alignment with God, and God is good!

Like Zen koans, this and the following verses seem designed to take the mind beyond its dualistic orientation and into full realisation of the non-dual nature of the Self.

8. I am neither the worshipper nor the object of worship. Neither instruction nor ritual exist for Me, for I perform no action. My nature is pure Awareness—so how can I speak of Myself? Freedom is My nature; maya does not pertain to Me.

9. No particular thing pervades, and no particular thing is pervaded. Neither the manifest world nor the unmanifest pertain to Me. How, then, can I speak of the visible and the invisible? Freedom is My nature; maya does not pertain to Me.

10. I am neither a perceiver nor an object of perception. I am beyond both cause and effect. How, then, can I speak of the conceivable or the inconceivable? Freedom is My nature; maya does not pertain to Me.

11. I am neither divided nor undivided. I am neither that which knows nor that which is known. How, then, could I speak of that which comes and that which goes? Freedom is My nature; maya does not pertain to Me.

12. I have no body, yet neither am I bodiless. I have neither intellect, nor mind, nor senses. How, then, can I speak of desire and desirelessness? Freedom is My nature; maya does not pertain to Me.

13. Nothing exists independently of the Self. One cannot speak of that which is nonexistent. How, then, oh friend, can I speak of the Self in terms of similarity or dissimilarity? Freedom is My nature; maya does not pertain to Me.

14. Neither have I conquered nor am I bound by the senses. "Should" and "shouldn't" are meaningless concepts to Me. How, then, oh friend, can I speak of "success" or "failure"? Freedom is My nature; maya does not pertain to Me.

15. I have neither form nor the absence of form; and I have no beginning, middle, nor end. How, then, oh friend, can I speak of "youth" and "agedness"? Freedom is My nature; maya does not pertain to Me.

16. Never have I been subject to death or deathlessness; nor evil or good. None of these opposites exist in Me, dear child. How, then, can I speak of "purity" and "impurity"? Freedom is My nature; maya does not pertain to Me.

17. Never have I experienced the states of sleep and waking or the heightened states of yoga. For Me, there is neither day nor night. How, then, can I speak of the transient states of mind? Freedom is My nature; maya does not pertain to Me.

States of consciousness are not experienced by the Self, but by the body-mind-sense complex. This apparatus is illumined and granted temporary life by reflected Consciousness, much as the moon is illumined by the reflected light of the sun. Like an eternal sun, the Self is the original Consciousness; the light by which all experience is revealed, while itself remaining free of experience.

18. Know Me as unaffected by the appearance or non-appearance of the world. I am unperturbed by either the presence or absence of maya. How, then, can I speak of the performance of prescribed action and ritual? Freedom is My nature; maya does not pertain to Me.

19. As one experiences in samadhi, all things are One. I, however, am unaffected by the attainment or non-attainment of samadhi. How, then, can I speak of union or separation? Freedom is My nature; maya does not pertain to Me.

Samadhi pertains to the mind, not the Self. The Self, as pure, unconditioned Consciousness is ever whole and free, illumining the mind just the same in all states of mind, however mundane or exalted.

20. I am neither ignorant nor learned. I neither observe silence nor do I speak. How, then, can I speak of that which is true or false? Freedom is My nature; maya does not pertain to Me.

21. I have neither father or mother, nor family or caste. I have never been born, thus I can never die. How, then, can I speak of affection or attachment? Freedom is My nature; maya does not pertain to Me.

22. I am, by nature, eternal and ever present. I am never affected by darkness or light. How, then, can I speak of rituals such as morning and evening prayers? Freedom is My nature; maya does not pertain to Me.

23. Know without doubt that I am limitless. Know without doubt that I am changeless. Know without doubt that I am untouchable by anything in this world. Freedom is My nature; maya does not pertain to Me.

24. Those with strong discrimination have no need for meditation. They renounce all their good actions along with the bad. They enjoy the sweet nectar of renunciation. Freedom is My nature; maya does not pertain to Me.

Indeed, discrimination—the ability to distinguish oneself, Awareness, from the shifting forms appearing in it—is intrinsic to liberation. All actions and their results are then viewed as the objects they are; and all objects relate not to the Self, but to Ishvara and the empirical world of maya.

25. For the Self, at the Absolute order of Reality, there exists no versified knowledge of any kind. But here, in this relative realm of samsara, I, the Avadhuta, have attempted to speak of this Supreme Absolute.

Here we have an acknowledgement of the paradox at the heart of the teaching. While Dattatreya has so poetically asserted the Self to be utterly free, beyond knowledge and ignorance, good and bad, and the presence or absence of the phenomenal world, these words are shared out of compassion for the suffering souls in samsara; those who have not yet ascertained their identity as the eternal, ever free Self.

Chapter 5

1. The syllable Om is the essence of That which pervades everything, rendering all distinctions between "this" and "that" irrelevant. The formless Unmanifest manifests as the world of form. How else could the Imperishable Self reveal Its light?

The syllable Om ("Aum") is used throughout the Upanishads as a symbol for the Self: the creative principle behind the cosmos and the essence of the creation itself. Called the *pranava*, it prefaces many of the great mantras of the Vedic tradition. Its repetition is a potent meditation in itself. As you chant Om, the key is to fix your mind on contemplation of your own nature as the limitless, all-pervading, deathless Self. This is what we call *Nirguna* Vedantic meditation; keeping the mind fixed on the formless, attributeless Self.

Given the difficulty the mind has in grasping the abstract, beginner or intermediate students often find it easier practising *Saguna* Vedantic meditation. This means meditating on the Self in the form of a personal deity, such as Krishna, Shiva, Ganesha, Kali, Buddha, Jesus, or whatever aspect of divinity you feel an affinity for and connection with. The greater you become at meditating on a concrete form of the Self, the easier it becomes to then contemplate the Self as the formless totality of All That Is.

2. "You are That" declare the scriptures. As the Self, I am free of the adjunct of maya and the same in all. Why do you grieve, then, O mind? I am the same Self in all.

The Upanishads offer a range of *mahavakyas*, or "great sayings", encapsulating the ultimate Truth of reality in just a few short but loaded words. *Tat Twam Asi,* "You Are That", is one of the most famous, along with *Aham Brahmasmi*, "I am Brahman (the Self)", and *So Ham,* meaning "I Am That". They all affirm our essential identity as being non-separate from universal Consciousness/Awareness/Existence.

A powerful form of Vedantic meditation is to continuously reflect on one or more of these statements of Truth until the knowledge gradually takes root in the mind. It's worth repeating that the entire aim of Vedantic teaching is to reorient your sense of identity from the limited and ultimately unreal body-mind-ego to the Infinite Light of pure Awareness or Consciousness. This doesn't happen by itself. The knowledge must be consistently and repeatedly applied to mind, over time transforming the mind's many layers of self-ignorance to Self-Knowledge.

3. I have no "higher" or "lower" and no "within" or "without". I am the One, all-pervading Self. Why do you grieve, then, O mind? I am the same Self in all.

The Avadhuta Gita makes seemingly paradoxical statements throughout its seven chapters. These are designed to help us see that, as the limitless and all-encompassing Self, our essential nature exists transcendent of duality and its pairs of opposites. These limitations pertain only to the relative order of reality and not the Absolute in which we have our true being. This idea is explored over and over in preceding and subsequent verses.

Each verse until the end of the chapter includes a closing

refrain exhorting the mind to relinquish its needless grief, which is based on ignorance alone—for we are the same Self, the same illuminating Awareness, enlivening all beings.

4. For Me, there is no distinction between the experiencer and that which is experienced; nor between the cause and its effect. Indeed, where is the distinction between a poem and its words? Why do you grieve, then, O mind? I am the same Self in all.

5. For the Self, neither knowledge nor ignorance exist. For the Self, neither near nor far exist. For the Self, neither time nor space exist. Why do you grieve, then, O mind? I am the same Self in all.

6. For the Self, there is no space inside a jar and no jar. There is no individual body and no individual soul. There exists no distinction between cause and effect. Why do you grieve, then, O mind? I am the same Self in all.

The scriptures often use the analogy of a clay jar for understanding the Eternal Self in relation to apparent self. While a jar might appear to be a separate, limited form, the space around and within the jar remains one. In other words, the jar is pervaded by space both within and without, just as the Self pervades all forms both within and without.

Dattatreya's assertion that there is no individual body or soul perhaps requires some analysis. For an individual body or soul to exist of themselves, they would have to possess their own separate, independent existence. This is impossible, because all forms are but manifestations of an underlying, fundamental cause—that being the Self; pure Consciousness. All forms have only a dependent, borrowed existence. The jar, for example, is simply clay plus a certain name and form ("jar"). It borrows its entire existence from the clay and doesn't exist independently of the clay. In much the same way, the individual body and soul, which we call the jiva, has no existence outside of Consciousness.

7. From the Self's perspective, all beings are eternally free. Time and definitions of "short" and "long" have no meaning, nor distinctions such as "fat" or "thin". Why do you grieve, then, O mind? I am the same Self in all.

The Self is already and ever free. By claiming your birthright and knowing, with the entirety of your being, that you are the Self, you attain freedom by realising that, but for the presence of ignorance in the mind, you were never bound.

8. Only the One exists; neither empty nor full, without purity or impurity, neither whole nor part. Why do you grieve, then, O mind? I am the same Self in all.

Vedantic scriptures often describe the Self as being full, whole and ever pure. Such statements are helpful for beginner and intermediate students. Ultimately, however, the Self is beyond description and categorisation. Part of the problem with labelling it as "this" or "that" is that, existing beyond the opposites of duality, it defies categorisation. The purpose of these verses is to negate that duality. For this reason, the Avadhuta Gita is considered one of the more advanced Vedantic texts.

9. No distinctions such as "divided" or "undivided" exist in truth; nor do distinctions such as "within" or "without". Beyond false divisions such as "friend" and "foe", I exist as the One Self. Why do you grieve, then, O mind? I am the same Self in all.

10. Ultimately, there is no student or teacher; no one is higher and no one is lower. At the Absolute order of Reality, the All is ever One and eternally free. Why do you grieve, then, O mind? I am the same Self in all.

11. The Self is neither with form, nor is it formless. It is beyond difference and non-difference. It is beyond creation and the absence of creation. Why do you grieve, then, O mind? I am the same Self in all.

If the Self is the Non-dual, limitless and divisionless totality of All That Is, it must necessarily encompass all that exists in both this manifest world of form and the undifferentiated Unmanifest. It is both day and night, the form and the formless, the unity and the multiplicity. It is, in truth, the only factor in existence.

12. Neither the gunas nor anything else can bind me. How can I be bound by actions in this life or the hereafter? I am the pure, stainless Self within all beings and forms. Why do you grieve, then, O mind? I am the same Self in all.

The gunas are the consistent elements of the material and subtle worlds; the three qualities that come together to create the worlds of form, much as the threads of cotton combine to form a shirt. The material world, and all the forms within it, appear within the Self, universal Awareness, yet the Self is ever unaffected by them, much as the dreamer is unaffected by the content of his or her dreams each night.

13. The Self pertains to neither existence nor non-existence; to desire nor desirelessness. The scriptures declare Self-Knowledge as the gateway to freedom. Why do you grieve, then, O mind? I am the same Self in all.

A seeming contradiction arises here, for we have already stated that the Self is synonymous with Existence. Dattatreya's point here is that, in its ordinary usage, existence is generally understood in relation to non-existence. Discrete objects such a pen, a cup, or a person enjoy only a finite, time-bound existence, for they borrow their limited existence from the timeless, infinite Self, which is the foundation and support of All That Is.

The most important point of Vedanta is reiterated here: namely that Knowledge of this Self, and one's non-difference from that Self, is the doorway to liberation. Again, the reasoning is simple: the Self is free, therefore, if I am the Self—and there's nothing else I can be, because nothing else exists—I must also be free. Of course, as simple as that is, it takes consistent effort to reorient the mind by fully integrating this basic truth. That's why the final stage of Vedanta, nididhyasana, is all about continually applying this Knowledge to the mind until it finally "gets the memo", so to speak.

14. The Self is neither divided into levels of existence or being; nor union or separation. Even in the absence of phenomenal reality, I remain the same Eternal Self underlying all beings and forms. Why do you grieve, then, O mind? I am the same Self in all.

15. The Supreme Reality, the Self, is not a vessel, house or sheath. The Supreme Reality, the Self, is beyond association or disassociation. The Supreme Reality, the Self, is beyond knowledge or ignorance. Why do you grieve, then, O mind? I am the same Self in all.

16. It is untrue to define the Self as either changing or unchanging. It is untrue to define the Self as either purposeful or purposeless. The truth is: the Self alone exists. Why do you grieve, then, O mind? I am the same Self in all.

Again, teachers often describe the Self as "changeless" or "unchanging", which is true. The problem with using such words to describe the indescribable is that it immediately calls to mind the opposites of duality. We can only really understand light in contrast to dark, pleasure in contrast to pain and the changeless in contrast to the changing. Duality relates only to the relative world; the world of forms and objects. As the limitless ground of Existence, the Self is beyond any measure of duality. The only true statement we can really make about it is: It *is*.

17. Every being borrows the same consciousness that is the Self. Every being lives as a reflection of the one Eternal Self. Only the one undivided Self exists. Why do you grieve, then, O mind? I am the same Self in all.

Just as the same sun shines upon all the reflective surfaces in the world, so does the same Self shine upon all the bodies and minds in creation, enlivening them each with reflected Consciousness. This Consciousness does not belong to those body/minds any more than the reflected sun belongs to the mirror or the water it is shining on. It is a borrowed light; a temporarily gifted sentience belonging to the one, Eternal Self.

18. The ignorant see difference in the undifferentiated. The ignorant doubt what is beyond all doubt. The wise see only the one, Eternal Self. Why do you grieve, then, O mind? I am the same Self in all.

19. For the Self, there is no liberation and no bondage; there is neither good karma nor bad. There is no state of perfection and no state of imperfection. Why do you grieve, then, O mind? I am the same Self in all.

20. If I am ever the same and beyond all division; if I am ever the same and beyond cause and effect; if I am ever the same and beyond differentiation, why do you grieve, then, O mind? I am the same Self in all.

As jivas, our misery stems from basic self-misconception; specifically, the sense that we are separate entities—meagre conglomerations of matter, mind and emotion, cut off from the rest of the creation and subject to karma both good and bad. What if that was never actually the case? What if it was only seemingly true? What if we shared our true identity with the very Source and Substance of all creation; the deathless and eternally pure Consciousness pervading the entire cosmos both manifest and Unmanifest? That's what the scriptures assert. Suffering comes from being out of alignment with this fundamental Truth about the very nature of our being. Liberation is claiming that identity as our own.

21. In Me, everything is eternal; everything is pure Consciousness. Here, the Truth is immutable; everything is pure Consciousness. Without exception, everything is pure Consciousness. Why do you grieve, then, O mind? I am the same Self in all.

If Consciousness alone exists, then nothing can exist apart from it. Everything must be that Consciousness—including "you" and "I". This truth is Absolute; no exceptions granted. Duality is nothing more than an erroneous belief in the mind.

22. Being eternal and indivisible, everything is my Self. Free from stain and attachment, everything is my Self. Without day or night, everything is my Self. Why do you grieve, then, O mind? I am the same Self in all.

23. Neither bound nor unbound, I am the unchanging Self. Experiencing neither union nor separation, I am the unchanging Self. Untouched by either knowledge or ignorance, I am the unchanging Self. Why do you grieve, then, O mind? I am the same Self in all.

24. In Me, time and timelessness have no meaning. In Me, the constituent components of materiality lose their seeming reality. Only the Absolute and unchanging Reality eternally abides. Why do you grieve, then, O mind? I am the same Self in all.

25. In Me, there is neither material nor immaterial; the gross and subtle are indistinguishable. Only the Eternal Self is ever the same; nameless and indescribable. Why do you grieve, then, O mind? I am the same Self in all.

26. Eternally pure, all-pervading and yet transcendent of form, I am the same Self in all. Whether manifest as form or unmanifest as the formless, the Essence is One. Why do you grieve, then, O mind? I am the same Self in all.

Some seekers have a hard time reconciling the notion that their innermost Self is the same Self in all beings. If that were true, they argue, wouldn't that mean that we ought to share other people's thoughts, memories and feelings? It's important to note that although the Self is the same, the instruments are many and varied. A good analogy is to think of electricity. The same electricity runs through and powers all the appliances in your house: from the lights, heaters and computer to the oven and toaster. In spite of this, the toaster doesn't "experience" the oven, nor does the ceiling lamp "experience" the fridge. These instruments are distinct and each function according to their respective design. The electricity, which is the real life behind them, enlivens each simultaneously, but it does not take on their qualities, nor is it in any way modified by the apparatus in question. So it is, too, with the Self and all the beings in the relative world.

27. As the Self, I am equally indifferent to virtue and vice, to the material and the immaterial, and to desire and dispassion. Why do you grieve, then, O mind? I am the same Self in all.

28. Unaffected by pleasure or pain, I am the same Self in all. Beyond both sorrow and joy, and neither guru or disciple, I am the one, self-existent Reality. Why do you grieve, then, O mind? I am the same Self in all.

29. Neither substantial nor insubstantial, the Self is neither in nor is it not in the material world. It exists beyond mental reasoning or lack of reason. Why do you grieve, then, O mind? I am the same Self in all.

It's incorrect to state that the a Self is "in" the material world, for that would render it subject to the limitations of materiality. Yet the material world could not exist without Consciousness; the Self being the underlying Existence/Reality of all things. It is more accurate to say that the material world appears "in" the Self, although even that statement is also subject to negation. It can be helpful to think of the material world as like a dream appearing in the mind (or, as the following verse states, a desert mirage). The dream world occupies a certain order of existence, otherwise it couldn't be experienced, yet its "reality" is completely dependent upon the consciousness in which it arises.

30. This Self is the underlying Essence of all names and forms. How can you find distinctions in this one Existence? It cannot be perceived by the senses as an object of perception. Why do you grieve, then, O mind? I am the same Self in all.

31. The scriptures have in so many eloquent ways declared this world of form to be nothing but a desert mirage, with only the Self as the one, indivisible, eternal Reality. Why do you grieve, then, O mind? I am the same Self in all.

32. Knowers of the Self have no use for versified knowledge, having realised the Self as the one, eternal Existence underlying all. But while apparently occupying the state of worldly existence, I, the Avadhuta, have shared this knowledge of the Self.

Versified knowledge means scriptures such as this. The Bhagavad Gita states that for those blessed souls liberated by Self-Knowledge, the scriptures are "as much use as a puddle when the land is flooded". When you know beyond a shadow of doubt that you are the Self, you have no further need of such words. When ignorance is gone and the mind is firmly established in this Knowledge, no further inquiry is needed. The nature of the teacher, however, is to teach, just as the impulse of the student is to learn. And so Dattatreya, the Avadhuta, has composed this text for the benefit of all sincere and qualified seekers.

Chapter 6

1. In so many eloquent ways, the scriptures have revealed the world of form to be nothing but a desert mirage. If there is only one, limitless and indivisible Self, everything is God. How, then, can this Self be compared to anything?

The very heart of Vedantic teaching is a vision of Non-duality; the knowledge that there is only one factor in existence—Brahman, or the Self: pure, undifferentiated Awareness or unconditioned Consciousness.

That being so, how can a separate world of form and objects appearing to exist independently of Consciousness? For anything to exist other than the Self, we'd have to inhabit a duality and the scriptures make it clear that, despite appearances, reality is one and undivided. The technical term for this is *advaita*, meaning "not-two".

Clearly, we do experience a world of objects with our senses and mind, so we can't say that it doesn't exist. Vedanta concurs that it exists, but points out that its isn't *real*. There's a difference. Something can exist without being real; the "blue" sky being a prime example. According to Vedanta, this universe of names and forms appears courtesy of maya, a Sanskrit term meaning "illusion" or "magic".

Maya is that which makes the impossible possible—that by which the one, formless, Non-dual Self appears as a manifold world of form and duality. As Dattatreya says in this verse, this gives the world the ontological status of a desert mirage. We can see and experience a mirage with our senses, but it's not actually there. It's a misperception of reality. Similarly, we may experience a universe of different forms and objects, all of it apparently separate from us, but this is simply the way that our physical senses structure reality for us. All that's actually here, and all that we're ever actually experiencing, is our own Consciousness. Why? Because, as the scriptures clearly state, reality is Non-dual and Consciousness is all that exists.

Understand this and you have grasped the very heart of Vedantic teaching. Because there is only one, indivisible Reality, which for lack of a better word we call the Self, everything is, therefore, Divine. The Avadhuta Gita uses the name "Shiva" as a synonym for this universal Consciousness. While in some verses I kept the translation as "Shiva", in the second line of this verse (which is repeated throughout the rest of this chapter) I changed it to "God", which perhaps has a more universal connotation.

Quite often even spiritual people take umbrage with the word "God", largely due to centuries of misuse at the hands of religion. A word is a word, however—a symbol pointing to a greater truth. While believers and non-believers argue relentlessly over the existence or non-existence of their conception of God, there's no room for debate in Vedanta—because, simply, nothing exists *but* God. For how can you have an effect (the world of form) without a cause (the formless) and how can that effect exist independently of its cause? That's why, as Dattatreya affirms again and again, "everything is God."

2. The Supreme knows neither division nor non-division. The Supreme knows neither activity nor inactivity. If there is only one, limitless and indivisible Self, everything is God. That being so, where is the need for austerities and religious rites?

Division and non-division relate only to this dreamlike world of maya; the universe of form and experience appearing to the mind and senses. The "Supreme" refers to the underlying and all-pervading Awareness in which this world appears: the beginningless, endless, unchanging Self that you (and all beings) are. It cannot be attained by action, for there was never any time it was non-attained. It is the essence and substance of all things. All that needs to be done is for the mind to be purified and re-conditioned to apprehend Reality as it truly is.

3. The Universal Mind is infinite and all-pervading; and the Supreme neither "without" or "within". As the Universal Mind is One and beyond limit, everything is God. How can it therefore be encapsulated in thought or word?

This and subsequent verses are short but potent meditations designed to strip away all sense of duality. This helps us recognise the underlying Non-duality that exists as the basis, heart and essence of everything; the one, indivisible substance in creation appearing to us as a manifold universe of objects and forms.

4. The distinction between day and night has no meaning for Me; nor does the distinction between dawn and dusk. If there is only one, limitless and indivisible Self, everything is God. What difference does it make if the sun or the moon are shining?

5. Beyond the duality of desire and dispassion, and beyond the duality of action and inaction, if there is only one, limitless and indivisible Self, everything is God. How meaningless, then, are the distinctions of "inside" and "out"?

6. Neither with substance nor without substance, neither a void nor non-void, if there is only one, limitless and indivisible Self, everything is God. How, then, could there be beginning or end?

7. Free of distinction between division and non-division; free of distinction between knower and known, if there is only one, limitless and indivisible Self, everything is God. How, then, can mental states pertain to It?

8. The ultimate Truth cannot be spoken in words. Neither what is spoken nor what is unspoken can encapsulate the Reality. If there is only one, limitless and indivisible Self, everything is God. How, therefore, can the Self be contained by form, senses, intellect or mind?

The Self, the ultimate ground and totality of Reality, cannot be described by words. Words are symbolic representations of reality; a crude shorthand allowing us to communicate information. How, then, can we explain Vedanta: a dualistic means of knowledge aimed at revealing this Self? To gain knowledge of what is, all we must do is remove our ignorance. Vedanta uses words to dispel self-ignorance. This ignorance binds us to the world of form by virtue of false identification with objects.

While Vedanta must necessarily use words to point to the Self, these terms are generally negative in nature, because we can only recognise the Self by negating what it is not. Thus, we might describe the Self as limitless, formless, timeless, unchanging and unbound by form and experience.

Self inquiry, which is key to Self-Knowledge, challenges us to examine this in the our own direct experience. We come to realise that we cannot *be* anything that we witness, such as the body, mind, thoughts or ego. These are all objects known to us. In order to arrive at the truth, we must be able distinguish between subject and object. The Self alone is the eternal subject; the light of our own Awareness; that by which all is known to us. This subject cannot be perceived as an object any more than the eye can see itself or a camera can photograph itself. Its existence, however, cannot be denied.

9. Neither space nor air are ultimately Real, nor earth, nor fire. If there is only one, limitless and indivisible Self, everything is God. How can one distinguish the raincloud from the rain?

All objects, all perceivable things, from the grandest of forms to the subtlest of elements, fall under the category of mithya, meaning apparently real. While objects appear to possess their own separate existence—"this" as distinguished from "that"—all phenomena, themselves time-bound effects, borrow their existence, or beingness, from an inseparable and underlying Cause at the heart of creation. That cause is called Satya, another name for pure Consciousness; the very essence of Existence, and our own innermost nature.

10. The Self is not contained by thought-based worlds; nor by thought-based gods. If there is only one, limitless and indivisible Self, everything is God. How, then, can it be affected by discrimination between the apparent and the actual?

The practise of discriminating the actual from the apparent, satya from mithya, is one of the most important tools in Vedanta's arsenal. By separating the objects from the subject, we are able to dis-identify from the components of the false self (specifically, the body, mind and ego) and reclaim our original and true identity as the Awareness in which they appear.

While this is crucial for the liberating the mind, this verse points out that such discrimination has no effect on the Self. The Self, after all, was never bound in the first place. It remains eternally free and untouchable by anything in this apparent world of creation. Just as the light shining on the cinema screen remains unblemished by the images projected into it, so does our innermost consciousness remain untouched and unmoved by both the inner and outer worlds experienced by the mind and senses. This is an important understanding. As the Self, you have never been bound in any way. Bondage is merely a product of ignorance and misperception of reality.

11. The Self is ever free of the duality of birth and death, and unaffected by action and inaction. If there is only one, limitless and indivisible Self, everything is God. How, then, can one speak of coming and going?

12. The material world and the Eternal Self are not separate, but one, just as the effect is inseparable from its Cause. If there is only one, limitless and indivisible Self, everything is God. How, then, can one speak of the Self and not-Self?

As noted above, the ability to discriminate between the Self and not-Self, or the subject and the objects appearing in it, is a key part of Vedanta's teaching methodology. Ultimately, however, it is only a tool to help students to get clear about the nature of Reality. As there is only one factor in existence—the Self; pure Awareness—there can't possibly be anything it is not. Therefore, the notion of "Self" and "not-Self" can be negated, because duality is nothing but a thought in the mind. The Self alone exists. There is nothing that isn't the Self, whether we consider the forms of the phenomenal world or the formless noumenon from which it arises. As this chapter's refrain emphasises, everything is this one, indivisible Self—everything is God.

13. The Self has no childhood, no misery, and no bondage to the gunas. If there is only one, limitless and indivisible Self, everything is God. How, then, can it experience childhood, youth or old age?

All living beings, enlightened and unenlightened alike, are subject to the three gunas, or forces, that comprise the field of creation: harmony, activity/passion and inactivity/indolence. These three factors condition not only our external environment in every respect, but also the instruments of our body, senses, mind and intellect.

While it is both possible and advisable to actively manage the proportion of these gunas in ourselves and our environment, the only way to fully transcend them is to know that, as the Self, we are already free of them and all the concomitant burdens, joys and sorrows of materiality. The light of our Awareness remains constant, eternally self-effulgent and untainted by anything in this apparent creation. While bodies undergo birth, ageing and death, Awareness remains changeless—and therein lies freedom. Even while, as jivas, we are bound by the world, at essence, as the Self, we remain free of it.

14. The Infinite cannot be bound by the stages of life or by social class. This Self is not a product of cause or effect. If there is only one, limitless and indivisible Self, everything is God. How, then, can it be declared either perishable or imperishable?

15. The Self is neither perishable nor imperishable; neither created nor uncreated. If there is only one, limitless and indivisible Self, everything is God. How, then, can it be defined in terms of mortality?

Only that which has a beginning can have an end. The Self was never born, so it can never die. It is the eternally self-shining Light of all lights; the very substratum of Existence in which universes rise and fall like waves dancing upon the shore. Forms come and go, but the Essence abides, forever unmoved and unmoving.

16. The masculine principle of purusha (spirit) does not pertain to the Self. The feminine principle of prakriti (matter) does not pertain to the Self. If there is only one, limitless and indivisible Self, everything is God. The opposites of duality and their interrelationship have no bearing on the Infinite.

17. If the Self is free of desire and aversion, and impervious to pleasure or pain, if there is only one, limitless and indivisible Self, everything is God. From where, therefore, comes the sense of "I" and "mine"?

Our everyday sense of "I", "me" and "mine" is a product of the *ahamkara*, or ego, which is part of the subtle body. This otherwise inert mechanism is enlivened and illumined by the reflected light of the "original I"—pure Consciousness. Thus, for the purposes of grasping this subtle understanding, we have the "original" Consciousness and the "reflected" Consciousness of the body-mind-sense complex.

A great analogy is the light of the sun and moon. The sun is, in this case, the "original" light and the moon the "reflected" light. This moon has no light of its own, but mirrors the reflected light of the sun. The reflected Consciousness teaching helps explain how there can be only one Self, but many apparent selves. Extending the metaphor, there is only one sun in our solar system yet this sun will appear in all the reflecting instruments in the world; the very same light appearing in every mirror, every pond and in every puddle and dewdrop. That's how the one is capable of appearing as many.

18. Is it not true that neither virtue nor vice have any bearing on the Self? Is it not true that neither bondage nor liberation pertain to pure Consciousness? If there is only one, limitless and indivisible Self, everything is God. What meaning, then, have thoughts of sorrow or happiness?

Vedanta is a teaching only for qualified students; people of intellectual and emotional maturity, who have learned to surmount the worst excesses of the ego and its many and often hidden layers of desire and ambition. One of the criticisms levelled at Vedanta by some critics is that it promotes a kind of dangerous moral relativity. They point to verses such as this, which basically state the Self is beyond good and bad as the worldly see it.

Such people do not understand Vedanta and have failed to the grasp the fundamental basis of the teaching. It is true that, as the Absolute Non-dual ground of being, Awareness knows no duality, and that includes all concepts of "right" and "wrong". The fear is that some people may hear this teaching and use it to justify their own violations of dharma, such as exploiting and abusing others financially, sexually or emotionally. This is called Spiritual Narcissism, wherein the ego co-opts knowledge of the Self and uses it as an excuse to satiate its own lower urges and lusts.

Knowledge of the Self is in no way a substitute for self control and living a pure and dharmic life. Mature students will have already assimilated the teachings on dharma, which underpin every facet of Vedanta. The scriptures state that dharma must come before all else, including enlightenment. This is something not understood by some who have intellectually grasped Vedanta's core tenets, and who hurriedly set themselves up as teachers, using that newfound power to take advantage of others. In so doing, such people not only create bad karma for themselves and their students, but also cast a bad light on the entire Vedantic lineage.

There is no escaping the fact that at this level of existence, the objective world, dharma—which means doing what is right and appropriate in each and every circumstance—is essential to the world and to all our lives. This is explored in great depth in the Bhagavad Gita, one of Vedanta's primary source texts. Dharma should only be ignored at one's peril. While the Self remains unaffected by anything in the world of form, at an individual level, the violation of dharma will very much affect the jiva and the lives of those around it.

19. No distinction exists between the sacred ritual and the one offering it. No distinction exists between the act of worship and that which is worshipped. If there is only one, limitless and indivisible Self, everything is God. Who, then, is there to seek reward for their actions?

It's for this reason that the highest form of worship is to realise one's unity with all that is; one's essential nature as pure Awareness. By negating duality, we break all false bonds with—and all divisions between—the things of the relative world. By recognising our Oneness with All That Is, we come to worship and revere all things, and this becomes our sacred offering to life. We treat all things and all beings with sanctity, love and respect. What higher worship could there be?

20. The Self exists free of both sorrow and happiness. The Self exists free of both pride and humility. If there is only one, limitless and indivisible Self, everything is God. Why, then, would the notion of attachment or non-attachment arise?

21. The Self knows neither delusion nor non-delusion. The Self knows neither greed nor desirelessness. If there is only one, limitless and indivisible Self, everything is God. Why, then, would the notion of discrimination or non-discrimination arise?

Believing yourself to be a jiva, an apparent-self living in a world of form and division, is the fundamental ignorance underlying the continuous suffering of samsara. Very simply, by identifying with the body, mind and ego, you become subject to their sorrows and limitations. Experiences, both good and bad, shape the fabric of your psyche, subjecting you to all kinds of conflicting emotions and relentless attachments and aversions. Lifting your sense identification from this limited, assumed self, to that in which the aggregates of body, mind and ego appear—the pure, unchanging Awareness by which they are known—liberates the mind from its assumed sorrows.

22. There has never been either "you" or "I". All talk of family or social division is fallacy. Truly, I am Shiva, the one Absolute and Supreme Self. How, then, can I worship and to whom should I bow?

23. The distinction between guru and student is but illusion, as is the guru's instruction. Truly, I am Shiva, the one Absolute and Supreme Self. How, then, can I worship and to whom should I bow?

24. The distinction between bodies is but imagined, as is the distinction between worlds. Truly, I am Shiva, the one Absolute and Supreme Self. How, then, can I worship and to whom should I bow?

The enlightened know all forms and beings to be but appearances in the one, universal and eternal Awareness/Consciousness that is the Self; different waves upon the same ocean of Eternity. They see through the illusion of multiplicity to embrace the whole of creation in its unity. All things become sacred and all beings worthy of worship.

25. The Self knows neither activity nor rest, for It is ever pure, unstained, and immovable. Truly, I am Shiva, the one Absolute and Supreme Self. How, then, can I worship and to whom should I bow?

26. The distinction between embodied and bodiless is but illusion, as is the distinction between "right action" and "wrong action", for neither exists. Truly, I am Shiva, the one Absolute and Supreme Self. How, then, can I worship and to whom should I bow?

Going back to the first verse, all things in the perceivable universe are but the play of maya; the creative energy that allows the one, undivided Self to appear as a world of form and division. The presence or absence of maya, of this manifest universe, does not affect the Self in any way. It ever remains the same, both immanent in that it is the form and substance of all things, and yet transcendent in that it is not limited or modified by those things. That's why it is always free, and why, by returning our deepest sense of identification to that Self, we ourselves can "become" free by realising that, but for thoughts of ignorance in the mind, we were never actually bound.

27. For the Self, at the Absolute order of Reality, there exists no versified knowledge of any kind. But while apparently occupying the state of worldly existence, I, the Avadhuta, have shared this knowledge of the Self.

Chapter 7

1. A tattered shawl from the side of the road may serve as garment for the liberated one, who is ever free of karma and devoid of both pride and shame. He will sit nakedly in an empty hut, absorbed in the pure, stainless bliss of the Self.

Ramana Maharishi, the great sage of Arunachala in India, was one of the most celebrated *mahatmas* (great souls) of the 20th century. His life beautifully exemplifies the life of the avadhuta, or liberated soul, as described here by Dattatreya. Following his enlightenment at age sixteen, Ramana became a renunciate, dressed in nothing but a loincloth and living in a cave for many years where he meditated more or less constantly, keeping his mind absorbed in the bliss and light of the Self.

Those who realise their nature as pure Awareness, and who then take the time and effort to actualise that knowledge and embody it in their lives, naturally lose their attachment to the things of the world. Even the greatest of luxuries, the finest of clothes and fastest of cars pale into insignificance when compared with the bliss of pure Consciousness.

The more we absorb the mind into its Source through Vedantic meditation and contemplation of the true nature of reality, the greater the bonds of doer-ship and karma fall away until we eventually know ourselves to be a non-doer and the stainless witness of all that is. Those with such Knowledge have neither pride nor any sense of insufficiency. They realise that the person they previously took themselves to be is but the play of the gunas.

Such beings derive their joy from the limitless well of Wholeness at the core of their being and never again know the crippling sense of lack and fear that blights the worldly.

The next few verses continue to explore how this liberated soul, the avadhuta, sees and relates to the world.

2. The liberated care not for attainment or non-attainment. Transcending the opposites of duality, they remain established in the the pure, stainless Reality. Why should such an Avadhuta feel impelled to either speak or refrain from speaking?

3. Free from bondage to the fetters of hope; free from the chains of ordained conduct; free from everything in this world, the liberated enjoy absolute peace, knowing themselves to be the stainless and ever pure Truth of Being.

4. For the Self-Realised soul, what difference does it make whether enjoying form or formlessness? Where is the worry of attachment or non-attachment? Such beings exist as the naked Truth of Reality, as infinite and boundless as the open sky.

5. Knowing the Supreme Truth of Reality, how can one speak of worldly knowledge and of form and formlessness? Outside the Supreme Self, as infinite and unbounded as the sky, how can a world of differentiated objects exist?

The essential truth at the core of Vedanta is that only pure Awareness/Consciousness exists. This Awareness has no limit, no boundary, and thus cannot be divided or modified in any way. In the last chapter we explained maya; the creative force that allows for a world of apparent form and duality to appear within this universal Consciousness. This world cannot exist separately or independently of the Self, for that would necessitate both limitation and duality, both of which are antithetical to the nature of the Self.

This world is, therefore, but a projection in Consciousness; the product of ignorance. The scriptures liken it to a rope which, in the murky twilight, appears to be a snake. We might see and experience a snake and react to it with visceral terror, but the snake is only a superimposition; a mirage created by the mind and taken to be real, even though it does not exist. The same, too, with this world of objects and form. We experience it as real and independently existent, when all that really exists, and all that we're ever actually experiencing, is Consciousness appearing as a universe of names and forms.

6. This Self is indivisible and undifferentiated like the formless sky; the one, pure and stainless Reality of all. How, then, can we explain difference and non-difference, bondage and freedom from bondage, division and change?

Duality, suffering and liberation pertain only to the jiva existing in the empirical realm of objects and form. As human beings, we are very much affected by worldly factors, and by physical and mental changes and challenges. As the Self, however—pure Awareness—

nothing in this world, or any other, can touch us in any way. Eternal, infinite and beyond duality, our very essence is stainless and pure. Like Teflon, nothing sticks to Awareness! No matter what changes and traumas the body and mind undergo, our true essence is changeless and undiminished in any way. Knowing this is freedom.

7. Reality is One indivisible Whole. This being so, how can there be union, separation, or notions of attainment? The Self is the Supreme, indivisible All; how, then, can there be either substance or lack of substance?

This verse again draws contrast between the world of the relative (the empirical world of names and forms experienced by the mind, body and senses) and the Absolute (the undifferentiated Awareness underlying those forms). When you find yourself caught up in thoughts of union and separation, attainment and loss, or any of the other opposites of duality, you can bet that you're identifying with the body-mind-sense complex and not as your true nature as Awareness. The Self just *is*; eternal, indivisible and whole. Nothing can be added to Awareness and nothing can be taken from it. Knowing this is freedom!

8. Only the One, stainless, indivisible Reality exists. Like the sky, it is clear, pure, formless and all-encompassing. How, then, can association or dissociation occur? In this One Reality, how can there be either relationship or the absence of relationship?

9. The enlightened one is a yogi who is free of yoga; an enjoyer who is free of enjoyment. Thus, they leisurely wander through life, their mind filled with the natural bliss of the Self.

In the space of a verse we move from talking about the universal Self to examining the personal self, or the jiva. The worldly spend their lives vainly seeking happiness and fulfilment in the world of impermanent objects. This never works out in the long run, but only the wise few are readily able to acknowledge that. With clear vision, these "awakened" few then devote their lives to seeking bliss inwardly by reeducating the mind with Self-Knowledge and rigorously applying it until the mind eventually yields.

Having then "attained" enlightenment (the actualised Knowledge that one is eternally whole, free and unaffected by the play of matter), such souls are free to move about the world, enjoying its pleasures without attachment and free of binding desire and aversion. They no longer demand that the world and other people provide them with happiness because they have found an altogether more secure and lasting happiness: the bliss of their own nature as pure, limitless Awareness.

10. If the worldly are bound by knowledge and ignorance, how can one attain freedom from duality and non-duality? How can a yogi be natural and free from attachment? By becoming aware that one is the stainless, ever pure Self, one shall enjoy unchanging bliss.

No solution to maya can be found within maya. The only solution to the problem of samsara, of existential suffering, is to realise that the true and essential part of yourself is already free. Enlightenment cannot be found by chasing experience, no matter how subtle and sublime. Experience is, by its nature, fleeting and finite, and the finite can never lead us to the Infinite.

While yoga is an excellent tool for purifying the mind and making it fit to accommodate Self-Knowledge, it cannot in itself bring enlightenment because no limited action is capable of yielding an unlimited result. Indeed, chasing after enlightenment experiences and grand cosmic epiphanies—while arguably better than chasing drugs, sex and rock and roll—is only likely to create attachment to such states.

Even spiritual attachments are a form of bondage. The one attachment that liberates is attachment to the ultimate truth of Reality: which is to say, keeping the mind fixed on the Knowledge that you are the ever present, ever pure, ever limitless Awareness/Consciousness in which all things appear. Because the Self never changes, its bliss is constant and imperturbable.

11. The Self is Destroyer, yet beyond destruction and non-destruction. The Self is Sustainer, yet beyond sustainment and non-sustainment. Indeed, how can substance and dissolution exist for the Absolute Reality? This Reality is changeless and all-pervading like the formless sky.

This verse makes reference to what Indian tradition calls the Trimurti, or the gods Brahma, Vishnu and Shiva; representing, in turn, the cosmic principles of creation, sustainment and destruction. While the Self doesn't actively participate in the universe of form, at the macrocosmic level, the Self, associated with the creative principle of maya, appears as Ishvara, or God; the creative principle by which the manifest universe of gross and subtle matter appears, exists, and then dissolves back into the unmanifest in cyclic waves.

At the Absolute order of reality, the Self remains changeless and infinite, while at the empirical level we experience a world of change and limitation, created and overseen by Ishvara, the organising Intelligence that makes this superimposed realm of objects and form possible. These two orders of reality exist simultaneously as cause and effect; the effect (Ishvara and the empirical realm) entirely dependent upon its unchanging Cause (the limitless Self).

12. Free from everything and forever united with the Self, the liberated are the All, and yet free of all. How could birth or death exist for the One Reality? How can meditation or lack of meditation impact the Self?

By knowing who you are—the limitless Eternal Self—you realise that you are both one with all things yet unbound by all things.

Alas, Knowledge of your unity with the Absolute doesn't confer omniscience. You won't suddenly be able to see and experience things from other peoples' perspectives or to read minds. That's because, for the duration of this incarnation in the phenomenal world, your knowledge and experience is limited by a particular *upadhi*, or limiting adjunct—which means you will continue to process reality through the instruments of your particular body and mind.

But just as a drop of water is, in essence, no different from the ocean, so, too, do you realise your oneness with the totality of life. Although the senses will continue to process life as a duality, you are liberated by the Knowledge that this is but appearance alone, much like the "snake" superimposed upon the rope. Knowing that Consciousness alone exists, and you are that Consciousness, you are no longer troubled by the things of the world, which you allow to come and allow to go as they may.

How can birth and death affect that which was never born in the first place? To the Eternal, the birth and death of bodies are no different to the birth and death of thoughts. Nothing you can do, or not do, can diminish your Self in any way.

13. This world of the senses is conjured as by magic, like the water of a desert mirage. Beyond all differences, and beyond all forms, only the one Self exists—indivisible and impenetrable.

This verse again likens the maya world (one definition of which is "magic") to a desert mirage; something that appears real to the dazed traveller, but which is nothing but an intangible projection of the mind. When you know you are Eternal Consciousness, you will see the world as little more than a passing mirage; perceivable to the senses, but ultimately fleeting and unreal.

14. Awareness itself is indifferent to all things–from the performances of rites and duties, to the attainment of liberation. Therefore, how can those who profess liberation be affected by either attachment or non-attachment?

The Self, pure Awareness, is the witnessing Consciousness, alike in both good experiences and bad, and unchanging even as the jiva moves between the states of waking, dream and deep sleep. Our reactivity and subjective interpretations come from the mind and its bundles of conditioning. These, in turn, inform our actions, shaping our desires and aversions. This leads to the formation of attachments which bind the jiva to action and reaction and the cycle of birth and death that is samsara. The liberated, however, by knowing the Truth at the very heart of Reality, live impartially as the Self, unswayed by either attachment or detachment.

15. For the Self, at the Absolute order of Reality, there exists no versified knowledge of any kind. But while apparently occupying the state of worldly existence, I, the Avadhuta, have shared this knowledge of the Self.

This was a tricky verse to translate, and is one that's repeated at the end of several chapters. It concludes with yet another admission that the Self requires no scriptures or "versified knowledge". How could It when It is the essence of freedom itself? The Self requires no knowledge because it is non-dual and without limit. Indeed, it is that by which all knowledge is known.

Of course, for the jiva living in the world of maya, it's a different story. While worldly people have no regard for or interest in such Knowledge, sincere seekers of truth and enlightenment must devote their lives to its attainment. Fortunately, the enlightened Sages and Seers of the ages have shared this Self-Knowledge with love and generosity of spirit for the benefit of all committed and qualified students. And so it is on this note of love that Dattatreya ends the Avadhuta Gita, his Song of the Liberated Soul.

Om Tat Sat.

www.ingramcontent.com/pod-product-compliance
Lightning Source LLC
Chambersburg PA
CBHW050254120526
44590CB00016B/2346